JESUS, HUMANITY
AND THE TRINITY

JESUS, HUMANITY AND THE TRINITY

A Brief Systematic Theology

KATHRYN TANNER

FORTRESS PRESS   MINNEAPOLIS

JESUS, HUMANITY AND THE TRINITY
A Brief Systematic Theology

First Fortress Press edition, 2001

Published in collaboration with T&T Clark, Edinburgh. Copyright © 2001 T&T Clark Ltd. All rights reserved. Except for brief quotations in critical articles or reviews, no part of this book may be reproduced in any manner without prior written permission from the publisher. Write: Permissions, Augsburg Fortress, Box 1209, Minneapolis, MN 55440.

ISBN 0–8006–3293–1

Printed in U.S.A.   AF 1–3293

For Beryl Satter
(who knows very little about Jesus and would like to keep it that way!)

'From his fullness we have all received, grace upon grace.'
(John 1:16, NRSV)

Contents

⊱✿⊰

Acknowledgments

My deepest debt of gratitude is to Iain Torrance whose invitation to give *The Scottish Journal of Theology Lectures* for 1999 became the occasion for this book. My thanks, as well, to his whole family, especially Morag, for the hospitality shown me during my stay in Aberdeen, and to the Department of Divinity at the University of Aberdeen for their patience and engagement with the lectures I presented there.

Quite a number of people read the lectures at short notice – even before their delivery – and I am deeply grateful for their collegial assistance and helpful criticism. Especially significant on both a personal and intellectual front were the responses of Amy Plantinga Pauw, John Webster, Marilyn and Bob Adams, Jim Griffiss, Bruce Marshall, Paul Griffiths, Adela Collins, Stephanie Paulsell, Eleonore Stump, Ian McFarland, James Buckley, David Tracy, Gene Rogers, Nick Healey, David Kelsey, Hilda Koster, Jan Pranger, Matthew Boulton, Mary Fulkerson, Chuck Mathewes, Joe Jones, the University of Chicago Theology Club, and the Duke/UVA Theology Consortium. While I have tried to address their concerns, many of them will have to wait for the much larger book I plan to write as a sequel. I am grateful as well to my trusty assistant, Gregg Taylor, who was available at a moment's notice for research and bibliographic help, and who prepared the index.

Some of the material in chapters 3 and 4 was produced under the auspices of William Schweiker's Lilly-funded colloquium on Property and Possession, and the Center of Theological Inquiry's Eschatology Project, respectively. I thank Trinity Press International for permission to reprint in chapter 4 some of my essay, 'Eschatology without a Future?' (found in *The End of the World and the Ends of God*, ed. John Polkinghorne and Michael Welker, 2000).

Introduction

In order to witness to and be a disciple of Jesus, every Christian has to figure out for him or herself what Christianity is all about, what Christianity stands for in the world. Figuring that out is the primary task of systematic theology. Systematic theology offers a vision of the whole, a sense of how to bring together all the elements of Christian involvement into unity around an organizing center or centers. This book is a contribution to such an effort, understood not as a bleak and dry academic exercise, but as an attempt to meet an essential demand of everyday Christian living.

Churchgoing, the confession of one's faith in Christ before the world, and the intention of living accordingly, are forms of witness and discipleship that, on the face of it, might not seem to require much cogitation of this wide-ranging sort about the nature of one's Christian commitments. That they do require it becomes clear when one considers how Christian life is made up of countless occasions in which one must decide the acts, beliefs and attitudes that really are in keeping with one's Christian commitments. Decisions about the political allegiances or economic lifestyles that are appropriate for Christians, about whether to pray in US public schools or pay your taxes or go to war, decisions about the direction of one's church's mission to the wider community (how, for example, to divide church coffers between institutional upkeep and service to the poor), decisions about the shape of worship life in the daily round and on contested issues (for example, should children be admitted to the Lord's table, should non-celibate gays be ministers?) – decisions like these are the stuff of Christian life; they arise continuously and inevitably the more Christianity is a way of life to rival others, displaying all the complexity, contingency, and historical vicissitudes of human life as actually lived. To the extent people make up their minds on the basis of their Christian commitments, doing so involves comparing possible courses of action, belief or attitude against a sense of what Christianity is all about. Is going to war, or making social outcasts full members of one's church, or dedicating church money to new parish buildings rather than community service, the Christian thing to do? That all depends on what one thinks Christianity fundamentally stands for.

There is no obvious, established answer to this question which simply being a Christian commits one to. Christianity, over the course of its two-thousand-year history and throughout the extent of its global reach, exhibits a great variety of answers; Christians are simply not of one mind on this most fundamental of theological questions. Answers vary of course with church affiliation. But church affiliation does not decide the matter. Answers vary with time and place, regardless. Epochs of Western church history, for example, can be divided according to the issues that mean the most for Christian commitment – the early church centering its Christian concerns on the status of Christ and the doctrine of God, the Reformation and Counter-Reformation on issues of justification and sanctification, contemporary Christians perhaps setting questions of social justice and inclusion into the center of their understanding of what Christianity is all about. Christians further divide on the way they address the central issues of their time. Some of these divisions become the impetus for different religious communions – say, the division between Protestant and Catholic. But in even a single religious communion in the same historical circumstances, disagreements inevitably arise – say, between Arminians and Synod-of-Dort Calvinists in the seventeenth century, or between Lutheran pietists (who stress conversion experiences and personal holiness) and their more scholastic compatriots (who stress the importance of assent to church teachings) in the eighteenth century, or between staunch adherents to the present Pope's theological directives and Latin American liberation theologians in the 1970s and 1980s.

Christianity is simply too complex a phenomenon to be an easy or obvious whole: its symbols and sacred texts are too multivalent and diverse; its beliefs too tension-filled (for example, monotheism combined with a claim for the divinity of Jesus); internal inconsistencies among its practices and beliefs as pronounced as in any way of life developing over time in the push and pull of real life struggles. Figuring out what Christianity is all about requires, therefore, intellectual effort, and intellectual effort of a primarily systematic sort: one must put together, unite into some interconnected whole, the disparate and often logically disjointed variety of things that Christians tend to think, feel, and do in and out of church.

This systematic effort requires one to select and highlight. Not everything that Christians are prone to say, feel or do is properly Christian and therefore to be included in one's sense of the whole. Some things are more important than others, the more important matters being that around which the less important revolves. It also requires one to develop the meaning of what one has committed oneself to (for example, what is presumed or implied by the beliefs one holds). One must further specify meaning in order to determine compatibilities or incompatibilities among the things that Christians are prone to feel, do and believe.

These tasks of selection and emphasis are the immediate ones that the everyday decisions of Christian life prompt. Decisions about how to carry on as a Christian are obviously selective – deciding that one course of action is the Christian thing to do means excluding the propriety of others – and obviously involve judgments of relative importance and value – some aspect of Christian life (for example, inclusive concern for the stranger) made to carry more weight than others (for example, worry about the purity of Christian worship) on the way to a decision. To make the ordinary decisions of Christian life is essentially to draw out the implications of what one believes and does as a Christian – it is a meaning generating activity.

But these kinds of intellectual effort are in service of a sense for the whole and the work it performs in Christian life; they feed that determination of the whole and this sense of the whole underlies all these more immediate decisions. Dropping or downplaying something that is or might be a part of Christian life, developing the meaning of one's belief in one way rather than another – such processes go to establish a fit among the various elements of a Christian way of life;

not everything can be fitted together and the meaning of the various aspects of Christian life determines in great part what can be made to fit with what. And it is that sense of how things fit together as a whole that guides these processes of selection, emphasis, and meaning generation on particular counts. For example, how well a course of action under dispute fits with one's understanding of Christianity (and therefore is to be accepted or rejected) is determined in great part by how one has already fitted together into some whole the variety of Christian beliefs and behaviors not currently under dispute. Should Christian wives forego their own needs to meet those of their husbands and children? A lot depends on whether self-sacrifice is an organizing center for one's understanding of Christianity as a whole and how, in making a whole of one's Christian commitments, one has brought apparent Christian norms of self-sacrifice together with those favoring an egalitarian concern for the fulfillment of all (in keeping, for example, with the idea that God loves and wishes to further the good of all God's children impartially). How that lack of self-concern on the part of wives is viewed – the meaning of it as either a saintly regard for others or submission to sinful inequalities in marriage relations – is also determined in great part by one's prior sense of Christianity as a whole (for example, by whether one organizes one's sense of what Christianity is all about around selfishness or oppression as the major problem that Christianity works to address).

Because what Christianity is all about is not a simple given of Christian commitment, each Christian is a potential contributor to the effort. Indeed, the historical, geographical and intra-church diversity of opinion I have mentioned should prompt each Christian to take up the challenge of making something of his or her own Christian commitments, rather than eschew such decision in the expectation that what Christianity is, has already been determined for one. To the extent one takes responsibility for the shape of one's own life as a Christian, I have implied, one must take responsibility for what one thinks Christianity is all about. In a constructive dialogue and intellectual contest with all those other Christians, past and present, who have been similarly concerned, one should make figuring out what Christianity is all about one's personal responsibility. One should offer up one's own way of making sense of Christianity as a whole, to be set in competition with the great variety of ways that Christians in the past and present, the world over, have engaged the same task.

While this is a challenge to be taken up by all Christians in the course of their everyday lives, academic theologians have their own contribution to make on the basis of their own special skills and training – as this book hopes to demonstrate. Besides having the time and space for ongoing intellectual inquiry, as an academic theologian I have at my disposal a broader than average knowledge of the diversity of ways that Christians have made sense of their Christian commitments, at least in the Western and (to a lesser extent) Eastern Orthodox churches, at the level of both popular and elite theological productions (for example, theology books by and for clergy or educated elites; as well as what historians and social scientists can uncover about the lives of the laity or Christians on the fringes of socio-political and church power).

Such knowledge of the vast array of ways that Christians in different times and places have made sense of Christianity as a whole might be paralyzing. Indeed, many academic theologians seem caught up in the historical morass, never able to steer their way through it so as to venture any bold theological statement of their own. Change, contest, and lack of consensus in efforts at Christian witness and discipleship, which are the undeniable conclusions to draw from any honest historical inquiry into Christianity, might suggest one is lost without a compass.

This knowledge – as I hope to demonstrate – can also, however, be freeing and empowering; it shows one, by historical instantiation, the variety of ways that Christianity can be put together and pulled apart for novel rearrangements, and at what real human costs. It uncovers the dangers of certain forms of theological construction while holding out models, borrowed from the past and elsewhere, for possible use in the here and now. It provides directions, then, for theological construction, but, because of the vast diversity of the record, without suggesting that any of this is forced on theologians hoping to address current needs and challenges to the faith in particular contexts.

Rather than, for example, suggesting a norm of conformity with the past, knowledge of the diversity of Christian self-understandings highlights the ambiguities of theological achievements, their often limited relevance to particular times and place, and their tendencies towards obsolescence. Any belief in the inevitability or fixity of a certain understanding of Christianity erodes before a sense for the flexible richness of so variegated a Christianity ever dissolving and resolving itself again into new organized wholes.

But this knowledge of Christian complexity also draws one beyond any easy confidence in the theological adequacy of speaking simply for and from the present situation. As the historical record shows, situation does not determine the direction of theological construction. In any one time and place, theological disagreement is as intense as across differences of time and place; and, rather than being in any one-to-one correspondence with a particular time and place, theological constructions tend to drift across them. Context provides, then, no sufficient direction for theological decision.

Indeed, knowledge of Christian complexity works generally to draw the theologian's viewpoint beyond the narrow confines of the present situation. So much of contemporary academic theology seems blinkered by current common sense and the specifics of a particular location; without availing oneself of a knowledge of what Christians have said and done elsewhere and at other times, what Christianity could be all about thins out and hardens, unresourceful and brittle. Knowledge of Christianity in other times and places is a way, then, of expanding the range of imaginative possibilities for theological construction in any one time and place, a way of expanding the resources with which one can work. Placing one's own efforts within this ongoing and wide stream, one grows in appreciation for the two-thousand-year, global history of efforts to say what Christianity is all about, for the theological insights that might be contained within that history or be working themselves out there. Reading it all together (to the degree and extent that the limitations of one's knowledge allow), as a single very complicated argument about proper Christian witness and discipleship, what can a theologian like myself get out of it?

Despite the complexity of the effort (to which I can only hint in the notes of chapters to come), I offer in this short book the kernel of my own attempt, on this historically-informed basis, to say what Christianity is all about. In a much longer book or books, I will develop the systematic theology I sketch here. As it stands, many crucial topics are left unaddressed (for example, the question of Christianity's relation to other religions); the ones that are addressed could use a much fuller treatment – paragraphs becoming chapters. In such short compass, I also cannot engage in the body of the text with the work of other theologians, past and present, and thereby show the critical decisions made in arriving at my own position. Nor am I even able to do much to situate my effort, in terms of my understanding of the needs of the time and place in which I work – midwest America at the dawn of the millennium in this odd, internet-connected, one-world global economy.

What I offer instead is the heart of the matter as I see it, with as much simplicity and elegance as I can muster. A purity of vision, but one with enough depth to ramify across a vast array of topics with unexpected and complex effects.

1

Jesus

This book sketches a systematic theology that centers on Jesus Christ and his meaning for life in the world. In this first chapter I recover strands of an early church account of Christ, which I rework significantly to address modern concerns with human agency and freedom and modern emphases on conflict and process in human history. The second chapter situates this Christology, and the way of being human that it implies, within the broadest cosmo-theological frame. In that way I establish contextually the intelligibility of these accounts of Christ and a graced human life, while laying out some of the many levels of relationship between God and creatures which any full systematic theology would have to engage. In the third chapter, I hazard some ethical and socio-political implications of my treatment of graced human existence; and in a final chapter – appropriately enough – I discuss the end of things in Christ.

At the heart of this systematic theology is the sense of God as the giver of all good gifts, their fount, luminous source, fecund treasury and store house. Like an 'overflowing radiance,' God 'sends forth upon all things . . . the rays of Its undivided Goodness;' 'the divine Goodness . . . maintains . . . and protects [all creation] and feasts them with its good things.'[1] In establishing the world in relationship to Godself, God's intent is to communicate such gifts to us. The

---

[1] [Pseudo] Dionysius the Areopagite, 'The Divine Names,' trans. C. E. Rolt, in *The Divine Names and The Mystical Theology* (London: SPCK, 1940), 94, 87; see the whole of the influential imagery in chapter 4.

history of the world is God's working for the fuller bestowal of such gifts, each stage of this history – creation, covenant, salvation in Christ – representing a greater communication of goodness to the creature and the overcoming of any sinful opposition to these gifts' distribution.

Corresponding to such stages of increase in gifts bestowed are changed relations with God. The world is perfected by being brought into closer relations with the God who perfects it. In union with God, in being brought near to God, all the trials and sorrows of life – suffering, loss, moral failing, the oppressive stunting of opportunities and vitality, grief, worry, tribulation and strife – are purified, remedied, and reworked through the gifts of God's grace.

In short, God, who is already abundant fullness, freely wishes to replicate to every degree possible this fullness of life, light, and love outward in what is not God; this is possible in its fullness only to the extent the world is united by God to Godself over the course of the world's time. Met by human refusal to receive from God's hands in God's own time, by the creature's efforts to separate itself and others from the life-giving fount of divine beneficence, met by the human refusal to minister God's gift-giving to others, this history or process of God's giving to creatures becomes a struggle, a fight to bring the graced kingdom of God into an arena marked by sin and death.[2] The struggle is won by the same means necessary for increase in gifts of grace: growth in unity with God.

The most general or abstract principles underlying this systematic vision are the following: firstly, a non-competitive relation between creatures and God, and secondly, a radical interpretation of divine transcendence.[3] The second principle, as we shall see, is the precondition of the first.

A non-competitive relation between creatures and God means that the creature does not decrease so that God may increase. The glorification of God does not come at the expense of creatures. The more

---

[2] This sense of sin (as a refusal to receive from God for the good of creation) and of struggle follow those of Irenaeus in his *Against Heresies*.

[3] For a more technically precise exposition of these principles than I can offer here, see my *God and Creation in Christian Theology: Tyranny or Empowerment?* (Oxford: Basil Blackwell, 1988), chapters 2 and 3.

full the creature is with gifts the more the creature should look in gratitude to the fullness of the gift-giver. The fuller the giver the greater the bounty to others.[4]

Similarly, connection with God does not take away from the creature's own dignity as the being it is. The greater one's dependence upon God, the more one receives for one's own good. As Karl Rahner makes the point: 'genuine reality and radical dependence [on God] are simply . . . two sides of one and the same reality, and therefore vary in direct and not in inverse proportion. We and the existents of our world really and truly are and are different from God not in spite of, but because we are established in being by God.'[5] The distinctness of the creature is thus the consequence of relationship with God as its creator; here difference is the product of unity, of what brings together, of relationship. The perfection of created life, the perfection of the creature in its difference from God, increases with the perfection of relationship with God: the closer the better.

This non-competitive relation between creatures and God is possible, it seems, only if God is the fecund provider of *all* that the creature is in itself; the creature in its giftedness, in its goodness, does not compete with God's gift-fullness and goodness because God is the giver of all that the creature is for the good. This relationship of total giver to total gift is possible, in turn, only if God and creatures are, so to speak, on different levels of being, and different planes of causality – something that God's transcendence implies.

God does not give on the same plane of being and activity as creatures, as one among other givers and therefore God is not in potential competition (or co-operation) with them. Non-competitiveness among creatures – their co-operation on the same plane of causality – always brings with it the potential for competition: Since I

---

[4] This kind of non-competitiveness as an affirmation of both God's gift-fullness and our bounty as recipients of God's giving is perhaps given clearest expression in the theology of Thomas Aquinas. John Calvin's theology is also notable for this sense that all we have is from God, so that the more we have the more we should be grateful to God as giver. In Reformation theology, however, this principle takes on a negative cast: worry that creatures will not thank God for all that they are deflates reveling in the gifts themselves. So, for example, Calvin, *Institutes of the Christian Religion*, ed. J. McNeil, trans. F. Battles, vol. 1 (Philadelphia: Westminster Press, 1960), Book 3, chapter 15, section 5, 793: 'because all his things are ours and we have all things in him, in us there is nothing.' See Tanner, *God and Creation*, 105–19.

[5] *Foundations of Christian Faith*, trans. W. Dych (New York: Crossroad, 1978), 79.

perform part of what needs to be done and you perform the rest, to the extent I act, you need not; and the more I act, the less you need to. Even when we co-operate, therefore, our actions involve a kind of competitive either/or of scope and extent. Unlike this co-operation among creatures, relations with God are utterly non-competitive because God, from beyond this plane of created reality, brings about the *whole* plane of creaturely being and activity in its goodness. The creature's receiving from God does not then require its passivity in the world: God's activity as the giver of ourselves need not come at the expense of our own activity. Instead, the creature receives from God its very activity as a good.

With these last remarks I am suggesting a principle of divine transcendence, which I define more precisely in terms of talk about God that avoids either simple identity or contrast with the qualities of creatures. I just gave a very general example of this principle at work: passivity with respect to God is not to be inserted into the usual contrast between passivity and activity that holds for creatures. Passivity before God is not the same as passivity as we understand it in relations among creatures; in relation to creatures, one cannot, as in relations with God, be active in virtue of being passive. Passivity with respect to God does not conform to any simple contrast with activity since one might be passive or active on the plane of created reality, in dependence upon, as the passive recipient of, God's gifts; simple passivity with respect to God tells you nothing either way. Or to make the point a little differently, a simple contrast between activity and passivity will not do for creatures' relations with God because no matter how active one is as a creature, one is never anything other than the recipient of God's active grace – God remains active over all.

If the technicalities of all this leave you reeling, just remember that God is not a kind of thing among other kinds of things; only if God is transcendent in that way does it make sense to think that God can be the giver of all kinds of things and manners of existence; and only on that basis, in turn – God as the giver of all gifts – does it make sense to think of a non-competitive relation between God and creatures.

What these two principles of non-competitiveness and divine transcendence mean becomes clearer when one sees the very particular and unexpected form they take in an account of the incarnation and its saving effects. I have expressed these principles in more general and abstract terms now in order to suggest their importance for more than Christology. These principles apply in a variety of ways to the whole range of relationships between God and creatures, not just to the highly distinctive relationship between God and humanity found in Christ, the range of relationships I sketch in the next chapter. They are a frame, then, for the whole God/world relationship.

When expressed in a general way, these principles also help make sense of the way some Christians at least have thought it best to talk about Jesus, going back to the Chalcedonian formulas, a manner of speaking that has become less and less intelligible in the modern West. The general understanding of the relation between God and creatures, which these principles adumbrate, provides, in other words, a context of intelligibilty for the incarnation. As Athanasius made the point very early on in the history of Christian thought: 'If then the Word of God is in the universe . . . and has united himself with the whole . . . what is there surprising or absurd if we say that he has united himself with man also. For if it were absurd for him to be in a body . . . , it would be absurd for him . . . either . . . to be giving light and movement to all things by his providence.'[6]

---

[6] 'On the Incarnation of the Word,' trans. A. Robertson, in *Christology of the Later Fathers*, ed. Edward Hardy (Philadelphia: Westminster Press, 1954), 95–6. Athanasius also affirms, as I do, that the general principles have their clearest exhibition in the incarnation, 97–8.

More recently, D. M. Baillie also argues in this way – that if one can see the intelligibility of God's working with humans in the matters of providence and grace, one can understand the incarnation; see his *God Was in Christ* (New York: Charles Scribner's Sons, 1948), esp. 111–18. The same sort of argument is found in Robert Sokolowski, *The God of Faith and Reason* (Washington, DC: Catholic University of America Press, 1982), 34–9: 'the distinction between God and the world serves to permit the other Christian mysteries to be thought of as mysteries and not incoherences' (37).

Rahner, in the *Foundations of Christian Faith* and in articles on Christology and creation throughout the *Theological Investigations*, also suggests a turn to the God/creature relation as a way of understanding a Chalcedonian Christology. See 'On the Theology of the Incarnation,' trans. K. Smyth, *Theological Investigations*, vol. 4 (New York: Crossroad, 1982), 117: '[in the incarnation] we can verify . . . in the most radical and specifically unique way the axiom of all relationship between God and creature.' And his 'Current Problems in Christology,' trans. C. Ernst, *Theological Investigations*, vol. 1 (New York: Crossroad, 1982), 162–6: 'If in the Incarnation the Logos enters into relationship with a creature, then it is obvious that the ultimate formal determinations of the Creator–creature relationship must also hold in this particular relationship' (163 n. 1).

See also Henk Schoot, *Christ the 'Name' of God: Thomas Aquinas on Naming Christ* (Leuven: Peeters, 1993), 183–5.

This is, indeed, the primary agenda of this chapter: to show how these general principles resolve Christological conundrums or puzzles. Problems that arise in thinking about Jesus as truly divine and truly human – especially contemporary problems – seem to have their source, most generally, in an inability to understand the two principles I have mentioned.

This is not to say that what Christians want to say about Jesus can be deduced from these general principles.[7] As we shall see in the next chapter, these principles apply in materially different ways across the spectrum of God's relations with us. One case is not reducible to another. New levels of God's gifts are not predictable from previous ones – for example, God's incarnation is not predictable from God's gift of existence to creatures in creating them or from God's gift of covenant fellowship with Israel. Using these principles to head off Christological conundrums also does not imply that Christological claims have their *genesis* in more general beliefs about God's relation to the world.[8] In fact, I think general claims about God's relations with the world came to be formulated as much in response to Christ as the reverse. Indeed, the general principles at issue (whatever they mean) are unlikely to be thought true of the world unless true of Christ: Christ is their proof. Finally, my procedure here does not mean that

[7] Along with the rest of the points made in this paragraph, this is a Barthian modification of the appeal to a general understanding of the God/creature relationship for help in understanding the incarnation. See the criticism of Rahner in a Barthian spirit made by Walter Kasper, *Jesus the Christ*, trans. V. Green (London: Burns & Oates, 1976), 51–2, 135–6: 'Anthropology is . . . the grammar which God uses to express himself. But the grammar as such is still available for a great number of pronouncements. It is concretely decided only through the actual human life of Jesus' (51). 'So it is possible to put in a plea for the justice of an anthropological . . . statement of the problem within the theological interpretation of Barth himself, and to interpret the anthropological structures as the grammar which God makes use of in a non-deducibly new way' (135–6). Kasper offers this as a criticism of Rahner, but I think that Rahner makes much the same point himself. See, for example, Rahner, 'Current Problems in Christology,' 162–6.

[8] See Rahner, *Foundations of Christian Faith*, 177, 179, 203, 207, 212, 229. Also, 'Christology within an Evolutionary View of the World,' trans. K.-H. Kruger, *Theological Investigations*, vol. 5 (London: Darton, Longman & Todd, 1966), 187: 'The historical nature of human and also metaphysical knowledge permits us in actual fact to formulate such a formal scheme (of a world process on the way to Christ) only because we already know about the fact of the Incarnation, all of which is possible only *post Christum natum*.' This epistemological primacy of Christ is expressed on an ontological front when Rahner speaks of human relations with God generally as 'deficient modes' of the primary Christological relation ('Current Problems in Christology,' 165).

Christology is *about* the general relation between God and creatures or even that Christology is about the general relation between God and creatures as they benefit from the grace of Christ.[9] This is so, once again, because the case of Christ has its own irreducible distinctiveness. It is not an instance of a general relationship found everywhere; it is not the highest point on a continuous grade of relationships between God and the world.[10] While what happens in Christ may be the center of a theological account of the universe from its beginning to its end, it is not such by being simply repeated elsewhere.

Now the major conundrum affecting modern Christology is prompted by a heightened sense in modern times of Jesus' humanity. Historical criticism, for one, highlights the man Jesus and saves him from the church's idealization of him. Historical criticism, because of its methodological agnosticism (if not atheism) can only uncover a humanity of Jesus continuous with the humanity of persons elsewhere. It digs beneath dogma, moreover, and any *a priori* reason Christians might have for elevating Jesus' humanity beyond our ken. Modern understandings of human life naturally infiltrate this treatment of Jesus' humanity – understandings of human life that stress our freedom and capacities for self-determination, the process and historically

---

[9] Here I diverge from D. M. Baillie and Karl Rahner, despite what I have learned from them (see n. 6 above). I am generally following Karl Barth's reservations about Baillie (et al.) in *Church Dogmatics* IV/2, trans. G. W. Bromiley and T. F. Torrance (Edinburgh: T&T Clark, 1958), 55–60. In criticism of Rahner on this score, see Walter Kasper, 'Christologie von unten?,' *Grundfragen der Christologie Heute*, ed. H. Fries, A. Halder, et al. (Freiburg: Herder, 1975): '[G]eht es darum, ob damit das Einmalige und Neue der Geschichte Jesu hinreichend zur Geltung gebracht werden kann. Kann denn mit diesem Ansatz die qualitative Einmaligkeit der hypostatischen Selbstmitteilung Gottes in seinem Sohn gegenueber der gnadenhaften Selbstmitteilung Gottes im Geist gewahrt werden?' (158). Rahner has a legitimate worry about separating what happens in Christ from the human experience of grace, but his solution assimilates the former too much to the latter.

[10] Despite the many nuances of Rahner's position, I am therefore contesting the apparently continuous character of the relationship that joins, for Rahner, what happens in Christ with what goes on throughout the whole of creation as the recipient of God's grace. There are qualitatively different levels to God's gift-giving to the world, one of which I am suggesting at its perfect reaches is the incarnation; Christ is therefore not, as Rahner says, merely the irrevocable and irreversible pledge, guarantee and climax of the movement from God to creatures and from creatures to God as that movement takes place throughout the world, from its very beginning, by virtue of God's grace. The problem with Rahner here, as I read him, is not so much that he collapses the grace of Christ into those graces, of a weaker sort, offered to creation as a whole, but that he assimilates those general graces too much to what happens in Christ – that is, creation generally and from the beginning has too much.

conditioned character of human lives, and the conflict and struggle that ensue especially when the shape of our lives together is at stake.

In a typically competitive understanding of the relation between God and the world, the more the humanity of Jesus is emphasized in modern Christologies the more the divinity of Jesus is downplayed. Jesus tends to become nothing more than a human model of compassion, justice seeking, and self-sacrifice, for our imitation. The Christologies of ancient Antioch return to favor in modern Christologies that make Jesus a specially graced man from birth.[11] Christologies that insist on the divinity of Christ in the strong incarnational sense of the Word become flesh are tarred in modern times with the brush of docetism: if the humanity of Jesus so clear to us makes it difficult to understand his divinity, the insistence on Jesus' divinity, so crucial to the early ecumenical creeds, must slight Jesus' humanity.[12]

In truth, there is evidence of that slighting of Jesus' humanity, from the time of the early Greek or Alexandrian theological traditions on, but not, I would argue, as much as one might think. Working from aspects of this long tradition of incarnational thinking – the early Greek Fathers up through the sixth century, Thomas Aquinas, Bonaventure, the Reformers, Karl Rahner, Karl Barth, and some contemporary figures of Eastern Orthodoxy are the major figures for me – one can recuperate the emphasis in the early creeds on the divinity of Christ, while reworking the classical Chalcedonian formulas for understanding the incarnation (for example, Christ has two natures and is one person or *hypostasis*) so as to place a modern emphasis on the humanity of Jesus and his significance for life in the world on modern terms.[13]

[11] Fine examples of such a position, worked out with great intelligence, are to be found in Friedrich Schleiermacher, *The Christian Faith*, ed. and trans. H. R. MacIntosh and J. S. Stewart (Philadelphia: Fortress Press, 1976), paragraphs 93, 94; and in John Cobb, *Christ in a Pluralistic Age* (Philadelphia: Fortress Press, 1975), chapter 8.

[12] For the common charge that the early creeds, especially on the 'orthodox' Alexandrian understanding of them, foster docetism, see, for example Rahner, 'Current Problems in Christology,' 155–61, 173; John Knox, *The Humanity and Divinity of Christ* (Cambridge: Cambridge University Press, 1967), 61, 62, 73, 87–8, 91, 96, 98; Baillie, *God Was in Christ*, 10–20; and Wolfhart Pannenberg, *Jesus – God and Man*, trans. L. Wilkins and D. Priebe (Philadelphia: Westminster Press, 1977), 291, 339 and n. 30.

[13] Other theologians attempt this – Barth and Rahner, for instance – but not with the particular spin I give to both major and minor issues. Some indications of these differences (and of my debts to them) are offered in these notes.

The key to solving the puzzle is the general soteriological viewpoint of God's gift-giving in ever increasing unity with God, a viewpoint that can be unpacked, as I have said, according to those two principles of divine transcendence and non-competitiveness. Most generally, Jesus is the one in whom God's relationship with us attains perfection. In Jesus, unity with God takes a perfect form; here humanity has become God's own. That is the fundamental meaning of incarnation, of God's becoming human. In keeping with the general idea that unity with God is the means of gift-giving to what is other than God (what I have expressed more abstractly as a non-competitive relation between what we have and what God has), the effect of this perfect relationship with God is perfect humanity, humanity to which God's gifts are communicated in their highest form. The point of incarnation is therefore, as it was for the early Greek Fathers, the perfection of humanity; this is a human-centered Christology just because it is an incarnation-centered one.[14] By way of this perfected humanity in union with God, God's gifts are distributed to us – we are saved – just to the extent we are one with Christ in faith and love; unity with Christ the gift-giver is the means of our perfection as human beings, just as the union of humanity and divinity in Christ was the means of his perfect humanity. United with Christ, we are thereby emboldened as ministers of God's beneficence to the world, aligning ourselves with, entering into communion with, those in need as God in Christ was *for us* in our need and as Christ was a man for others, especially those in need.

This general viewpoint on Christology suggests how a principle of non-competitiveness is worked out here, but it does little as it stands to unpack (*a*) the meaning and intelligibility of incarnation, (*b*) the process by which its effects on humanity are achieved, or (*c*) the character of those effects as exhibited in Jesus' life. How, for example, might any of this respect the real humanity of Jesus, as that appears from the perspective of modern historical consciousness? Clearly quite a number of Christological conundrums remain for discussion in this chapter, keeping in mind the principles of divine transcendence and non-competitiveness I have mentioned.

[14] This is perhaps most obvious in the writings of Cyril of Alexandria; see his *On the Unity of Christ*, trans. and intro. John McGuckin (Crestwood, New York: St Vladimir's Seminary Press, 1995).

The first puzzle is simply the intelligibility of God's becoming incarnate. How is it that God can do this, without its coming at the expense of the very divinity that is the source of our salvation? The main problem here is the sense that God cannot become or be united with what God is not; it seems that characteristics of God are simply opposed to those of human beings – immutability vs. change, simplicity vs. complexity, infinity vs. finitude, etc. Incarnation, understood as becoming something one is not, would seem then to require either the loss of divinity or humanity – substantial change to one or the other. If incarnation simply means, as I take it, God's taking on of the human, its assumption as God's own, it is still the case that incompatibles seem impossible to unite, impossible to make one without real change to reconcile them.

Modern resolutions of the incarnation problem therefore tend either towards kenoticism or towards historicizing God.[15] In the former, kenoticism, God gives up, hides, or hinders the operations of God's own nature in order to be incarnate. In the latter view – of an historicized God – God is defined by many of the same characteristics that hold of human life, for example, temporality; God becomes Godself in and through our history. In both cases, the difference between God and humanity is attenuated in the incarnation, and thereby the soteriological importance of Jesus' divinity is altered for the sake of greater intelligibility – the incarnation makes sense but the point of it for us is harder to see. God must be incarnate in order to save, but God must be different from us in order to save us and it is just that difference that now seems jeopardized by kenoticism and the historicizing of God. God as an essentially historical being may now suffer along with us in Jesus, but how consoling is that? Why think, in

---

[15] On kenoticism, a mainly Lutheran movement with origins in the sixteenth century and a powerful proponent in Thomasius in the nineteenth, see the fine critical discussion of Pannenberg, *Jesus – God and Man*, 307–23; for more recent developments in Germany and Britain (for example, Charles Gore and Frank Weston), see the discussion of John Hick, *The Metaphor of God Incarnate* (Louisville, Kentucky: Westminster Press, 1993), 61–79; and Thomas Weinandy, *Does God Change?* (Still River, Massachusetts: St Bede's Publications, 1985), chapter 4.

Theologians prone to historicize God are, in the main, either Germans influenced by the legacy of Hegel – for example, Pannenberg, Moltmann, and Jüngel – or British and American process theologians, following Alfred North Whitehead.

any case, that God must be ignorant of our predicament or uncaring apart from the incarnation? If God's powers are not in evidence in the incarnation, as kenoticists think, in virtue of what are we saved?

Behind the problem, to which *kenosis* and the historicizing of God are offered as solutions, is the mistaken idea of God as a kind of being over against other kinds of beings – a mistaken view of divine transcendence to which my own is a counter. On my view, God is not simply opposed to the characteristics of human beings but beyond any such contrasts. It is that very radical transcendence that enables incarnation with what is other than God:

> The reason the pagans could not conceive of anything like the incarnation is that their gods are part of the world, and the union of any two natures in the world is bound to be, in some way, unnatural, because of the otherness that lets one thing be itself only by not being the other. But the Christian God is not a part of the world and is not a 'kind' of being at all. Therefore the incarnation is not meaningless or impossible or destructive.[16]

Rather than coming at the expense of divinity, incarnation is the very thing that proves divinity. As Gregory of Nyssa said in his *An Address on Religious Instruction*: '[T]hat the omnipotent nature was capable of descending to man's lowly position is a clearer evidence of power than . . . to do great and sublime things. . . . [D]escent to man's lowly position is a supreme example of power – of a power which is not bounded by circumstances contrary to its nature.'[17] Only what is not a kind – and therefore not bound by the usual differences between natures – can bring together in the most intimate unity divinity and humanity. Because divinity is not a kind, God is not bound by apparent contrasts between divine and creaturely qualities; God is thereby free to enter into intimate community with us, without loss to the divine nature, without sacrificing the difference between God and us. As Karl Barth puts it:

> We may believe that God can and must only be absolute in contrast to all that is relative, exalted in contrast to all that is lowly, active in contrast to all suffering, inviolable in contrast to all temptation, transcendent in contrast to

[16] Sokolowski, *God of Faith and Reason*, 36.
[17] 'An Address on Religious Instruction,' trans. C. Richardson, in *Christology of the Later Fathers*, ed. Edward Hardy (Philadelphia: Westminster Press, 1954), 300–1. See also his 'Against Eunomius,' trans. W. Moore and H. Wilson, *Nicene and Post-Nicene Fathers*, vol. 5 (Peabody, Massachusetts: Hendrickson Publishers, 1994), Book 5, chapters 3 and 4, 175–9.

all immanence, and therefore divine in contrast to everything human. . . . But such beliefs are shown to be quite untenable, and corrupt and pagan, by the fact that God does in fact be and do this in Jesus Christ. . . . By doing this God . . . shows Himself to be more great and rich and sovereign than we had imagined. . . . He is absolute, infinite, exalted, active, impassible, transcendent, but . . . He is all this as the Lord, and in such a way that He embraces the opposites of these concepts even while He is superior to them. . . . His particular . . . presence . . . in the man Jesus . . . is itself the demonstration and exercise of His . . . perfection. . . . His omnipotence is that of a divine plenitude of power in the fact that (as opposed to any abstract omnipotence) it can assume the form of weakness and impotence and do so as omnipotence, triumphing in this form.[18]

The distinction between substance and *hypostases* in the Trinity helps make the same point. This distinction is a way of indicating that the *hypostasis* of the Word, who becomes incarnate, is not restricted by its own substance or nature.[19] Without loss to itself, it may take on a created nature, a human one. This is possible for the *hypostasis* of the Word most fundamentally because, again, the divine substance is not defined, as finite substances are, by a nature exclusive of others.

It is the very transcendence of God, then – a transcendence beyond simple contrasts – that enables intimate union with creatures like humans. What makes God different from creatures is also what enables God to be with what is not God rather than shut up in self-enclosed isolation. True for Thomas Aquinas, according to Henk Schoot, as it is for Barth:

> God is not transcendent in the sense that he needs a difference to be the unique one he is. God is not different within a certain genus, on the basis of a common similarity. . . . God is 'outside' of any genus, and thus God is not different from creatures the way in which creatures mutually differ. God differs differently. . . . Such an account undermines the opposition between transcendence and immanence, because God is not transcendent in such a way that he is simply 'outside of' or 'above' the world, and thus not transcendent in such a way that it would exclude his 'descent' into the world.[20]

---

[18] *Church Dogmatics* IV/1, trans. G. W. Bromiley and T. F. Torrance (Edinburgh: T&T Clark, 1956), 186–7. See also 129–30, 158–9, 179–80, and the explicit reference to Gregory of Nyssa on 192. See also Karl Barth, *Church Dogmatics* II/1, trans. G. W. Bromiley and T. F. Torrance (Edinburgh: T&T Clark, 1957), 467 and 517.

[19] See Thomas Aquinas, *Summa Theologiae*, trans. Dominican Fathers (Westminster, Maryland: Christian Classics, 1981), IIIa, Q. 3, A. 1, ad 2; and M.-V. Leroy, 'L'union selon l'hypostaste d'après S. Thomas,' *Revue Thomiste* 74, no. 2 (April–June 1974): 228, 235.

[20] Schoot, *Christ the 'Name' of God*, 144–5.

Because God differs differently, the characteristics that distinguish God from creatures need not be covered over or held in abeyance, God's characteristics need not be made more like those of our common life, for God to be brought near to us, indeed to become one with us.

Immanence and transcendence, closeness and difference, are simply not at odds in God's relations with us. What makes God different from us enables closeness with us, as I have just said. And closeness, from God's side, establishes difference. Rather than taking away our difference from God, God's giving to us in relating to us is the very thing that brings about the difference between us; God's relating to us, God's coming near, is what gives us ourselves in our distinctiveness. This is true in God's creating of us – God's decision not to be alone but to be with what is not God brings about the existence of the creature distinct from God – and it is true in every other case, inclusive of the incarnation.

To put this point about closeness and difference in trinitarian terms, God is different from the world in virtue of the fullness of God's trinitarian life, but it is this very fullness that enables God to overflow in goodness to us.[21] The Father already brings about what is different – the Son and the Spirit – in complete unity with the Father. The triune God is therefore being nothing other than Godself in unity with a world different from God, as that unity and differentiation find their culmination in the human being, Jesus, who is God's very own.[22] 'Primarily and originally it is not the cosmos or man which is the other, the counterpart of God . . . [but] God is all this in himself' so that 'everything the creature . . . offers – its otherness, its being in antithesis to Himself – ' is God's own 'superfluous overflow.'[23] '[A]t the core of His being . . . God is the One who seeks and finds relationship. . . . He is Himself, and therefore to

[21] See the way Bonaventure exposits in a trinitarian fashion a Dionysian principle of divine self-diffusion in creation, according to Ewert Cousins, *Bonaventure and the Coincidence of Opposites* (Chicago: Franciscan Herald Press, 1978), 105–7, 237, 254.

[22] I use traditional trinitarian terms in this book for lack of a better non-sexist alternative that would enable me to make the same ultimately patristic theological moves. I believe there may be such functional alternatives but developing and defending one is a complex task that cannot be attempted in a book of such short compass.

[23] Barth, *Church Dogmatics* IV/1, 201.

everything outside Himself, relationship, the basis and prototype of all relationship.'[24]

More particularly, the Father is the source of difference in creative relationship with the non-divine world as a kind of extension outside God of the way the Father is the source of the Son and Spirit within the Trinity. The Father creates the world and sends the Son to us in Jesus and the Holy Spirit to dwell in us through Jesus – all as a kind of extension outside God of the way the Father is the source of the Son and Spirit within the Trinity. The Son is the image of the Father – all that the Father is in differentiation from the Father – so the world is the image of the Son in virtue of the Father's relations with the world through the Son – created through the Son, saved through the Son of God become Son of Man.[25] The Holy Spirit in the Trinity, pushing beyond the dyadic self-enclosure of Father and Son, opens that Trinity outward to what is other than God. Reinforcing the unity of being between Father and Son by a unity of love and joyful affirmation, the Holy Spirit is the exuberant, ecstatic carrier of the love of Father and Son to us. Borne by the Holy Spirit, the love of the Father for the Son is returned to the Father by the Son within the Trinity; so the triune God's manifestation in the world is completed in Christ through the work of the Spirit who enables us to return the love of God shown in Christ through a life lived in gratitude and service to God's cause.[26]

Finally, incarnation without attenuation of God's transcendence is no impossibility if one keeps in mind its soteriological, this-worldly point for life in the world – and avoids speculation, unhelpful and

---

[24] Barth, *Church Dogmatics* II/1, 641.

[25] Bonaventure and Barth, for example, put an emphasis on the second Person of the Trinity, or Son, as that trinitarian aspect of God's own transcendent being that makes possible God's relations with the world.

Note that here and throughout this book I use the terms 'Son of God' and 'Son of Man' as names that refer to Jesus under the description of divinity and humanity respectively. This is the theological use of the terms common since the patristic era; it does not correspond to their biblical use. See, for example, on the New Testament use, E. P. Sanders, *The Historical Figure of Jesus* (London: Penguin, 1993), 161–2, 173, 246–8.

[26] Eastern Orthodox theologians often put an emphasis on the Holy Spirit as that aspect of God's own transcendent, trinitarian life that opens it outwards to what is not God. See, for example, Dumitru Staniloae, *Theology and the Church*, trans. R. Barringer (Crestwood, New York: St Vladimir's Seminary Press, 1980).

unwise, concerning its meaning for God.[27] God is not changing God's relation to us in Christ but changing our relation to God. In the old language of the ancient church, God is not going anywhere when God becomes human; we are being brought to God, assumed into the divine trinitarian life.[28] God is doing what God is always doing, attempting to give all that God is to what is not God. We are not able to receive all that much simply as creatures, or even as God's covenant partners, certainly very little as sinners *per se*, without God's help overcoming sin and its effects. Only when we become God's own in Christ can our lives reflect, in a way appropriate to us, the complete communication of God's gifts that transpires among the members of the Trinity, who receive all because they are all equally divine.

Now, if this much is granted – that incarnation is a possibility for a transcendent, triune God – the question still remains, how it is possible for Jesus to be both human and divine at once? Despite what Chalcedonian talk of two natures might suggest, one should not try here to divvy up the life of Jesus into its divine and human qualities, to figure out where Jesus' humanity ends and his divinity begins, as if human and divine qualities were part of a continuous series or laid out on a continuum. Given God's transcendence, divine and human qualities are not differentiated like this, they are not comparable in keeping with any simple difference in kind.[29] One should not, then, search for divine characteristics of Jesus alongside his human ones – say, in omniscient awareness of the secrets of people's hearts or prevision of future events – characteristics that are the bane of historical criticism. Divine omniscience is not something like human knowledge, just better, minus the ignorance or the limitations of finitude; accounts of Jesus' omniscience, as a psychological matter, de-divinize omni-

---

[27] I am here disagreeing rather sharply with a trend in contemporary theology associated with Jürgen Moltmann.

[28] See, for example, Cyril of Alexandria, 'Scholia on the Incarnation of the Only Begotten,' trans. John McGuckin, in his *St Cyril of Alexandria: The Christological Controversy* (Leiden, E. J. Brill, 1994), section 4, 297–8.

[29] One of the best criticisms of the two natures language of Chalcedon on this score is found in Schleiermacher, *Christian Faith*, paragraph 96. See also R. A. Norris, 'Toward a Contemporary Interpretation of the Chalcedonian Definition,' in *Lux in Lumine*, ed. R. A. Norris (New York: Seabury Press, 1966), 78–9; and Pannenberg, *Jesus – God and Man*, 284–5, 287, 322.

science, make it into something like a human characteristic. Besides violating the principle of divine transcendence – indeed, because of it – when divine and human qualities are set next to one another they are set in competition: in the respects to which Jesus is divine (for example, omniscient) it is hard to see how he is still human, and the reverse. If one is leery of allowing divine qualities to simply replace their human counterparts in Jesus – following Chalcedon, Jesus is not partially divine and partially human but fully both divine and human – the result is a nonsensically redundant duplication of qualities – for example, Jesus is omniscient in so far as he is divine and ignorant in so far as he is human at the very same time – with all the difficulties that brings for establishing Jesus as a coherent character.

Better to think of divinity and humanity not in terms of isolable, discrete qualities that divide up Jesus' life and person, but as what characterize Jesus' life overall, as a whole. Jesus' life as a whole is both divine and human but on different levels or planes of reality, one being the source of the other. Jesus leads a fully human existence but this existence is the result of the assumption of Jesus' humanity by the Word. Because they occur on different planes, so to speak – the leading of a human life on a horizontal plane, the assumption of this whole plane of a human life by the Word on a vertical plane – they neither supplement nor replace one another. The same human features and effects of Jesus' life may be attributed to Jesus as both divine and human since Jesus' divinity, the Word's assumption of his humanity, is the immediate source of his whole human life. Jesus' compassion for the outcast, for example, has its human source – in presumably the historically conditioned human process by which he reached the decision for that course of life – and it has a divine source in the Word's assumption of humanity which gives human existence with this shape in its totality. In this manner Jesus can be said to lead a life both human and divine at the very same time.

When divinity and humanity are attributed to Jesus' life as a whole in this way, one is less inclined to discuss Jesus' two natures in abstraction from the soteriological point of what the triune God is doing in Christ, less inclined, for example, to become (mistakenly) preoccupied with fascinating, but ultimately beside-the-point issues concerning the exact relations between Jesus' divine and human qualities (say, how his divine omniscience and his limited human knowledge interact – might he tell himself as man what he knows as God?). Talk of two natures is instead brought back to the concrete events of salvation that such talk is supposed to illuminate. The point of two natures talk is now evident in what God does for us – assumes humanity – for the sake of human life, in order to bring about the sort of human life that Jesus lived.[30]

Discussion of the human and divine natures of Christ becomes more dynamic and more concrete by way of their reference to an actually existing person. Jesus is divine and human in that Jesus is both God becoming human and the human becoming divine. Jesus is divine because in him God becomes human – that is, God assumes the human. Jesus is perfectly human, the deified human, because in him the human becomes God – that is, the human is assumed by God so as to produce an elevated and perfected human way of life. Both at once – God become human and the human become God – because the second, the living of a perfectly gifted human life, is the direct result of the first – God's becoming one with the human.[31] Jesus is both the Word incarnate and deified or exalted humanity because these are just different descriptions of the same process from different points of view – the one highlighting the agency of the Word in uniting itself with humanity; the other coming at the same process from the flipside of its effect, humanity assumed and thereby perfected.

Notice that as a characteristic of Jesus' life as a whole rather than a particular, isolable quality, the divinity of Christ has a kind of invisibility: divinity makes no obvious appearance in the form of some identifiable empirical or metaphysical feature of Jesus' life. The second Person of the Trinity's assumption of the human is as invisible as God's acting to create and uphold the world: it transpires silently, behind the scenes; it makes no appearance in itself but is identifiable only in

---

[30] This effort to tie up 'two natures' talk with what is going on in Jesus' life is typical, for example, of Martin Luther's Christology; see Ian Siggins, *Martin Luther's Doctrine of Christ* (New Haven, Connecticut: Yale University Press, 1970). It is also crucial for Karl Barth's: see, for example, *Church Dogmatics* IV/2, 74–6, 98–9, 105–9.

[31] See, in Karl Barth's terms, the way the exaltation of the human *is* the humiliation of God's becoming human, considered in its effects on the human; *Church Dogmatics* IV/1, 132–5; and IV/2, 110–12, 117.

and from its effects. Rather than being a matter of direct perception or simple identification, the divinity of Jesus becomes an inference from the character of Jesus' life and its effects.[32] 'If a man should wish to see God, who is invisible by nature and not seen at all, he may know and apprehend him from his works.'[33] 'Christ is the image of the invisible God [the Father] even in respect of his invisibility: for if the [divine] substance of Christ were discernible, how could He be the image of an invisible nature?'[34] It is for this very reason that the affirmation of Jesus' divinity must be inferred. Although one cannot identify anything empirically or metaphysically out of the ordinary in them, Jesus' person and acts are nevertheless so out-of-the-ordinary as to be called divine, because they have a character and consequences exceeding any mere creature's capacities. In order to lead this sort of life and death, in order for this life and death to have the sort of saving effects on others that it has, one must be God, and work by the power of God. Thus, Jesus, to all appearances and as far as any metaphysical inquiry can tell, weeps and feels terror before death just as any human would: what is odd is the way Jesus overcomes these anxieties and fears – for example, the way he nevertheless conforms his will to the Father's as the Father's own Son would – and the saving consequences of such acts – Jesus overcomes our weeping and terror by weeping and being terrified.[35]

---

[32] One can defend, then, the divinity of Jesus, rather than merely assume it, with reference to the historical Jesus and the effects of his life on others. This takes the question of Jesus' divinity off the usual epistemological plane to which it is put in contemporary theology (by, for example, Pannenberg whose whole book *Jesus – God and Man* is premised on the idea, mistaken I believe, that traditional Christologies merely assumed the divinity of Christ without argument). Contrary to much contemporary theology, one is not, in other words, assessing the church's belief in the divinity of Christ by investigating how it developed, with good cause or not, from the evidence provided by Jesus' own life and self-understanding. One is instead asking more directly whether what Jesus was and did justifies the claim of divinity; this is less an epistemological question (about the justification of the church's belief by way, for example, of an account of its genesis) than an objective or 'ontological' question about the relationship between Jesus' person and acts and their preconditions.

[33] Athanasius, 'On the Incarnation,' 107; see also 72, 86.

[34] Hilary of Poitiers, 'On the Trinity,' trans. E. Watson and L. Pullan, *Nicene and Post-Nicene Fathers*, vol. 9 (Peabody, Massachusetts: Hendrickson Publishers, 1994), Book 11, section 5, 204.

[35] See Athanasius, 'Four Discourses against the Arians,' trans. J. H. Newman and A. Robertson, *Nicene and Post-Nicene Fathers*, vol. 4 (Grand Rapids, Michigan: William B. Eerdmans, 1957), 424.

To say that Jesus works by the power of God is not to say that Jesus as a psychological or metaphysical matter avails himself of divine powers, for example, uses his omniscience or decides to employ his miracle-working capacities. Jesus is simply human on that level; nothing like those divine faculties or powers are uncoverable by, say, closer empirical inspection or better historical investigation, or cleverer metaphysical analysis. It is rather to say that, for example, Jesus acts *as if* he is omniscient (meaning by that, that his acts are the sort of thing only an omniscient God might do for our benefit) despite the fact that as a human being he clearly is not.[36] Because what Jesus is and does is impossible for a mere human being, one attributes divinity to him; that simple attribution, without further specification in terms of empirical or metaphysical qualities, respects the transcendence of God. Developing an empirical or metaphysical account of those qualities would, that is, make them into either quasi-divine human faculties or divine powers comparable to human ones (for example, distinct from human powers by degree).

In another sense, however, the fact that Jesus' divinity is not located on the level of particular empirical or metaphysical qualities means his divinity is apparent *in* his human acts, rather than alongside them.[37] Jesus' divinity is invisible in and of itself – the assumption of the human as a divine act does not take place on the human plane – but that divinity nevertheless appears in the shape of Jesus' life. Jesus lives out in a fully human form the mode of relationship among Father, Son and Spirit in the Trinity.[38] The human shape of Jesus' life is not something alongside Jesus' divinity but the manifestation of that divinity as a human whole.

> It is only when . . . we find his divinity *in* his humanity, not . . . plainly visible over against it, but as operative in and through it, that we are on the right track. This means, then, that the judgment that Jesus is divine is . . . made in consequence of the experience of what he is and does, as well as what he was

[36] There are hints of this position in Athanasius and Hilary of Poitiers (see nn. 33–5), despite their tendencies to say the reverse: that Jesus knows everything and just hides the fact for saving purposes.

[37] See Rahner, 'Current Problems in Christology,' 190–1.

[38] See, for example, how Zachary Hayes explicates Bonaventure's views to make this point in *What Manner of Man?*, trans. with commentary by Zachary Hayes (Chicago: Franciscan Herald Press, 1989), 77–81, 86, 94.

and did. It is a total evaluation of the significance of his *whole* life, not a description of certain isolated areas of that life which are not really human but in some contra-human sense divine.[39]

Because the shape of Jesus' whole human life is the out-working of God's own trinitarian life, Jesus is not simply the means to what the triune God wants to give to us out of its fullness; the shape of Jesus' life is the end or goal of that giving, which we are to receive in union with him. Jesus, as the human version of the Son in his relations with Father and Spirit, is the means by which we are to receive the Spirit and be transformed thereby in our own humanity, but this Spirit is the Spirit of Christ who therefore works to conform us with the Son: our lives in and through the Spirit are to take on the shape of Jesus' own.

The invisibility of the divine as such in Jesus, as anything distinct from Jesus' humanity, means, too, that the uniqueness of Jesus is not to be sought in particular features of Jesus' life that one could identify as divine – for example, his unusual self-consciousness or psychology as a man with a perfect God-consciousness or his omniscient knowledge or even moral holiness. What is unusual about Jesus – what sets him off from other people – is his relationship to God (his relationship to the Word who assumes his humanity as its own), the shape of his way of life (as the exhibition of the triune life on a human level), and his effects on others (his saving significance). Jesus is not then distinct from others in any way that would jeopardize his human nature. His human nature is simply human; what is different is its source – Jesus lives in so far as he is God's own – and its concrete shape or mode.

Now what I have said so far about the humanity and divinity of Jesus might suggest nothing more than the usual solution to God's working with creatures who work: the same human effects might have both God and human causes or conditions behind them, as total causes each in their own order of causality, in that God is the immediate creative source of all that the human is and does.[40] But to affirm this

---

[39] W. Norman Pittenger, *The Word Incarnate* (London: James Nisbet & Co., 1959), 129–30; I do not agree with how Pittenger develops the implications of this for his own theological position.

[40] For more on this, see Tanner, *God and Creation*, chapter 3. This is the position of Thomas Aquinas, as I read him (see esp. *Summa contra Gentiles*, Book 3), but one can also find clear statements of the position in Bernard of Clairvaux, *On Grace and Free Choice*, trans.

general sort of *concursus* (or accompanying) of God with humans (to
use the medieval terminology) is to say less than Chalcedon: in Christ,
attributions of divinity and humanity are not only compatible because
everything with a human cause also has a divine one; here humanity
and divinity are attributed to one and the same subject; this same one,
Jesus, is both God and a human being. To put this difference from
general divine *concursus* another way: here the effect of divine agency
is not external to divinity, not separable from it, but something that
remains the divine's own. The same one Jesus Christ can therefore be
called either a human being or God, he can be indicated using names
that connote either divinity or humanity, he can be called either the
Son of God or the Son of man. These identifying descriptions are
convertible – just as 'the Word incarnate' (God become human) and
'the deified human' (the human become God) are for the slightly
different reasons indicated above. To put the difference from general
divine *concursus* in still another way: unlike the usual case where God
works with creatures who work, as the creative source of their own
working, here God's doing and human doing are not alternative
descriptions adequate as they stand within their respective planes; both
descriptions are necessary to discuss what is happening in Jesus' life,
what Jesus does on the human plane – for example, Jesus does not
save us simply as a human being nor simply as God, though the power
to do so is from God.[41] Instead, Jesus performs divine works in a human
way (saves us by living a human life); and performs human works in a
divine way (lives a human life in a way that saves). Thus, a human
being's dying on a cross is not saving unless this is also God's dying;
and God's dying does not save us (it is not even possible) unless God
does so *as* a human being.

This unity of subject, the unity of the one who is both God and a
human being, distinguishes Jesus from simply a specially graced
human being (though Jesus is also that); it indicates that Jesus is more

D. O'Donovan (Kalamazoo, Michigan: Cistercian Publications, 1988), 106; and in Karl
Barth, *Church Dogmatics* III/3, trans. G. W. Bromiley and T. F. Torrance (Edinburgh: T&T
Clark, 1960), paragraph 49, section 2.

[41] See Richard Norris' introduction to *The Christological Controversy*, ed. Richard Norris
(Philadelphia: Fortress Press, 1980), 30–1.

than a person whose character and effects require the exercise of God's power. Jesus is not simply a human singled out to exhibit and perform what only God can do.[42] He is not simply the conduit of divine power but someone who is himself both God and a human being. If he were not both, Jesus' human way of being would not be itself saving, but an accidental covering for the working of God. God would save by a kind of arbitrary fiat rather than in the gracious way of like saved by like: fallen humanity drawn away from its predicament by the human itself.[43] Contrary to such views, one must say 'God did all this, not merely through a man, for He was born of Himself, He suffered of his own free will, and died of Himself. He did it also as man.'[44] If he were simply a graced human being, that grace would also be merely an external gift to him, like the gifts of grace to ordinary human beings, and not part of his very constitution; those gifts might therefore be lost, as they are always prone to be lost by ordinary human beings, Christ providing in that case no new, more secure stage of God's graciousness but the return to an earlier one.[45] Nor would it make sense to worship Christ as Christians do. For soteriological reasons, then, one should follow the early ecumenical creeds in their affirmation of a single subject, who is both God and a human being.

But what accounts for this unity of subject? Here is a mighty conundrum! One should not look for this unity as a product of Christ's different natures – human and divine – as if the two might be mixed up so thoroughly as to become one.[46] On my way of looking at things,

[42] As, for example, Knox in *The Humanity and Divinity of Christ* (59–60, 81, 107, 109–10, 113–14) thinks.

[43] This is a common refrain especially in the early Greek church, see, for example, John of Damascus, 'Exposition of the Orthodox Faith,' trans. S. Salmond, *Nicene and Post-Nicene Fathers*, vol. 9 (Peabody, Massachusetts: Hendrickson Publishers, 1994), Book 3, chapter 1.

[44] Hilary of Poitiers, 'On the Trinity,' 157.

[45] This is also a common position in the early Greek church. See, for example, Athanasius, 'On the Incarnation,' 99.

[46] Aloys Grillmeier sees this conclusion as one of the major achievements of the first six centuries or so of Christological controversy; see his *Christ in the Christian Tradition*, vol. 1, trans. J. Bowden (Atlanta: John Knox Press, 1975). Unity does not take place on the level of the two natures but on the level of *hypostasis* (to use the Chalcedonian language). This is the position of Maximus the Confessor and John of Damascus, for example. For the latter see, 'Exposition of the Orthodox Faith,' Book 3, chapter 8. In contemporary theology this is the position of Rahner; see his 'Current Problems in Christology,' 180–3. See also Barth, *Church Dogmatics* IV/2, 65–6, 70.

the divine nature is not comparable enough to a human nature to make much sense of their being combined into a unity anyway. But assuming they were sufficiently comparable, these natures seem so different that a genuine unity arising out of them seems out of the question. If they were to be made one, some mixture, some third thing with a new combined nature, would likely result, making Jesus less than fully divine or human. Or the natures might form a single one by supplementing each other – as the soul needs the body and the body the soul – but that suggests deficiency rather than fullness on one side or the other. A thorough co-inherence or interpenetration of natures that remain themselves – the old example of heated iron comes to mind – is the best hope, but it is not enough to ensure unity here, where, unlike the case of the trinitarian Persons, the natures that interpenetrate are different, and it is unlikely the co-inherence is fully mutual. (Jesus' humanity may be fully suffused with the divine; but the Word's being fully suffused with the human is a much more controversial claim, involving a denial of a Logos apart from Jesus. Even the former case is problematic, encouraging insistence on something like Christ's resurrected life – the glorified humanity of Christ – before the crucifixion.) When fire makes iron glow, the fire and the iron become one in virtue of that fact in only a highly attenuated sense: they are really two as their separate existence before and after such an occurrence attests.[47] A non-substantialist meta-physics, such as one finds in process philosophy, is no solution: it may successfully show how a unity results from the combination of divine and human but it does so at the expense of Christ's divinity. For example, Jesus may be constituted as a person by his perfect response at all times to the divine lure of the Logos or creative transformation, but divinity in this case is simply a kind of thing within the world.[48]

'*Hypostasis*,' for all of them, does not ensure unity as a static category; it is the level on which the active uniting of the Word with humanity takes place – the *hypostasis* of the Word takes humanity to itself in Jesus. See, for example, Rahner, 'Current Problems in Christology,' 182 n. 1. More on this in my own text below.

[47] See John of Damascus, 'Exposition of the Orthodox Faith,' 55–60.

[48] See Cobb, *Christ in a Pluralistic Age*; divinity becomes the power of creative transformation in the world.

While divinity and humanity are brought together in Jesus' life –
otherwise it makes no sense to talk about Jesus' acts as saving or the
character of his own life as exalted by God beyond what human powers
are capable of – it is best not to look there for an explanation of the
unity of Christ's person as both God and a human being. One should
seek an explanation instead in the divine cause of the togetherness of
divine and human functions in Christ. The unity of Christ's person
has its explanation in God's uniting with the human – in God's
becoming human. The unity of Christ as both God and a human being
follows from the specific way that God unites with the human here; it
follows from the fact that here the humanity that God gives rise to
remains God's own. Because everything about Jesus' humanity is
God's own, when one refers to the human being Jesus, one refers to
God (and because of that fact, what God has is, in turn, Jesus' own, it
is communicated to Jesus).

There are different ways in the history of Christian theology to make
this point about everything about Jesus' humanity being God's own.
In the early church, one might simply talk, as I often do, with little
increase in intelligibility, of the Word assuming or taking humanity to
itself.[49] One might talk with Karl Rahner of Jesus as the symbol or
self-expression of God, or of God's quasi-formal rather than efficient
causality with respect to him.[50] Thomas Aquinas makes the point by
speaking of humanity as the Word's proper instrument, something
like an extra hand or finger – in contrast to an axe, external to the
Word and employable by another.[51] Aquinas also talks about Jesus
achieving the status of a concrete something to which one could
attribute predicates only in the way a transplanted organ might,
existing in another, and in that way its host's own.[52]

---

[49] See, for example, Cyril of Alexandria, *On the Unity of Christ*, 59, just one among many
others passages, following the famous Cappadocian formula that what is not assumed is not
healed. See also Ruth Siddals, 'Logic and Christology in Cyril of Alexandria,' *Journal of
Theological Studies* 38, part 2 (October 1987): 341–67, for the way Cyril also uses the language
of 'property' to make the point.
[50] See Rahner, 'The Theology of the Symbol,' trans. K. Smyth, *Theological Investigations*,
vol. 4 (New York: Crossroad, 1982).
[51] See Thomas Aquinas, *Summa contra Gentiles*, trans. C. O'Neil (Notre Dame, Indiana:
University of Notre Dame Press, 1975), Book 4, chapter 41, sections 11 and 12.
[52] See on this, M.-V. Leroy, 'L'union selon l'hypostaste d'après S. Thomas,' 224–6.

The early church distinction between the anhypostatic and enhypostatic existence of humanity in Christ, revitalized and refined by Karl Barth, is another way to make this point about a unity of subject or who, a way of making the point that I favor.[53] Apart from his existing in the Word, Jesus has no existence of his own; this is what it means to say that Jesus' humanity is anhypostatic: abstractly considered, that is, considered apart from the Word, Jesus has no existence as a human being. Jesus exists only in God's Word; that is what it means to say Jesus' existence is enhypostatic in the Word: Jesus *has* a human existence but only in virtue of having his existence in God. Jesus does not just get his existence *from* God, as we do; he exists in God; his very existence is God's existence. When referring to the Word incarnate one therefore refers to the human being Jesus and when referring to the human being Jesus one refers to the Word.

Notice here how the unity of person and the difference in natures have the same explanation; they converge on the same process by which God keeps as God's own the humanity that God effects as different from itself. The uniting and differentiating powers of the Word, exhibited in the process by which God becomes human, are what reconcile the unity of Christ's person with the duality of his natures.[54]

In what sense is the Word the one subject of all that Jesus does and suffers? The one, Jesus Christ, is properly referred to by names connoting either divinity (Son of God) or humanity (Son of man) or both (for example, the Word incarnate). But rather than leave it at that, the interpretation of Chalcedon that won out in both East and West preferentially identified this one, both truly divine and human, with the Word.[55] How is that compatible with the obvious fact – so

---

[53] See Karl Barth, *Church Dogmatics* I/2, trans. G. W. Bromiley and T. F. Torrance (Edinburgh: T&T Clark, 1956), 136–8, 148–50, 160, 163–5; and *Church Dogmatics* IV/2, 49–60, 90. See also Hans Stickleberger, *Ipsa assumptione creatur: Karl Barths Rückgriff auf klassische Christologie und die Frage nach der Selbständigkeit des Menschen* (Bern: Peter Lang, 1979), 157–8; for trinitarian parallels, see Thomas F. Torrance, *The Trinitarian Faith* (Edinburgh: T&T Clark, 1988), 221, 226, 230, 327.

[54] See Rahner, 'Current Problems in Christology,' 181.

[55] See Anthony Baxter, 'Chalcedon, and the Subject in Christ,' *Downside Review* 107, no. 366 (January 1989): 1–21, for the point that Chalcedon itself does not identify the one subject with the second Person of the Trinity; an unambiguous creedal identification of that sort awaits the Second Council of Constantinople in 553. I do not agree with Baxter that such an identification is a mistake.

obvious to modern people – that Jesus is a human being? Well, we have said that Jesus *is* a human being; this one, this who, the particular human being Jesus, is the effect of the Word's making humanity its own – it is just that this one is not external or separable from the Word's own existence. The ultimate or preferential identification of this subject with the Word is simply a way of indicating the primacy of the Word's active agency for all that transpires here.[56] God becomes human and the human becomes God, but the latter only as the result of the former – that primacy of the Word's agency, the primacy of the Word's doing for our salvation is what the preferential identification of Jesus with the Word signals. What remains obvious, however – all that remains obvious on the level of empirical or metaphysical description – is the human being Jesus, his life as the effect, inseparable though it might be, of the Word's primary agency throughout.

The usual Cyrillian/Alexandrian discussion of the Word's doings in Jesus – 'the Word said or did this or that' – is therefore an anthropomorphizing of the Word, whenever it threatens to push aside the effects of the Word's agency on the human plane: here, it is the human being Jesus who genuinely acts, discourses, and suffers.[57] Since this particular human being and the Word are one, it is certainly also true that the Word does and suffers all that – there would be nothing saving to Jesus' life otherwise – but the Word does not do and suffer them as a human being would, in a fashion like that of a human being, forming opinions, taking action, moving one's lips to speak, disguising one's omniscience, etc. To think so is to bring divinity down to the human level; it is to be untrue to the apophatic emphasis otherwise so characteristic of these same theologians. That the Word is the subject here simply means that what Jesus does is attributed to the Word in the same way the Word's own properly divine predicates are attributed to the Word; the human being Jesus acts but these are God's own works.

This fully human life of Jesus exhibits the usual historical conflicts and historical processes of human life as we moderns conceive it. Although the deification of humanity is just the flipside of God's

---

[56] See, for example, Barth, *Church Dogmatics* IV/2, 62–3.

[57] For examples of an apparent anthropomorphizing of the Word, see Cyril of Alexandria, *On the Unity of Christ*, 103, 105–6, 110.

assuming the humanity of Jesus for God's own, that deification does not happen all at once, but over the course of Jesus' life and death.[58] God's making the humanity of Jesus God's own is an all or nothing affair, but what is assumed and its effects on human life are not. As Jesus' life and death proceed, all these various happenings are made part of God's assumption of the human, with purifying, healing, and perfecting effects. Each aspect of Jesus' life and death, moreover, is purified, healed and elevated over the course of time, in a process that involves conflict and struggle with the sinful conditions of its existence.

The purification and elevation of the human in Christ is a historical process because the humanity assumed by the Word is historical.[59]

By his intimate union with humanity, [Christ] shared all the marks of our nature. He was born, reared, grew up, and went so far as even to taste death. . . . [I]t was in keeping with his intimate union with our nature that he should be united with us in all our characteristics. . . . That is why, in view of the fact that our life is bounded by two extremities (I mean its beginning and end), the power which amends our nature had to reach to both points. It had to touch the beginning and to extend to the end, covering all that lies in between.[60]

The modern affirmation of the essentially historical character of human life simply makes this all the clearer, though the recognition of such an historical nature is also sometimes strongly affirmed in the very early church, notably by Gregory of Nyssa.

The purification and elevation of the human in Christ is a conflictual process because the humanity assumed by the Word suffers from the effects of sin.[61] Contrary to what is commonly affirmed in the medieval period, with Karl Barth and some early church fathers (Athanasius, Gregory of Nyssa, Hilary of Poitiers, John of Damascus), one must say that the Word assumes, not a perfect humanity (if the humanity

[58] See, for example, Gregory of Nyssa, 'An Address on Religious Instruction,' 303–4; and Athanasius, 'Four Discourses against the Arians,' 422. See also Hilary of Poitiers, 'On the Trinity,' 213–17, for the way at least the body of Jesus is sanctified over time, though not in any linear way.

[59] See John Meyendorff, 'Christ's Humanity: The Paschal Mystery,' *St Vladimir's Theological Quarterly* 31, no. 1 (1987): 22–30; Rahner, 'Current Problems in Christology': 'The Logos did not merely become (statically) man in Christ; he assumed a human history' (167); and Barth, *Church Dogmatics* IV/2, 140.

[60] Gregory of Nyssa, 'An Address on Religious Instruction,' 304.

[61] See Karl Barth, *Church Dogmatics* IV/3, trans. G. W. Bromiley and T. F. Torrance (Edinburgh: T&T Clark, 1961), 166–8, 197.

assumed were already perfect, what would be the soteriological point of assuming it?), but humanity suffering the effects of sin – tempted, anxious before death, surrounded by sufferings of all kinds, in social conditions of exclusion and political conflict.[62] The Word's assuming or bearing of all this in Christ means a fight with it, a fight whose success is assured by that very unity of the human with the Word, but a genuine fight nonetheless where success is not immediate but manifests itself only over the course of time.

The incarnation is not, then, to be identified with one moment of Jesus' life, his birth, in contradistinction from his ministry, death and resurrection. The incarnation is, to the contrary, the underlying given that makes all that Jesus does and suffers purifying, healing and elevating. As I have said, the incarnation is a given but what is being assumed and the effects of that assumption vary over time. The humanity of Jesus is therefore not perfected from the first as an immediate consequence of the incarnation, making Jesus' struggles and sufferings something he merely decides to go along with (a merely 'economic' matter, as patristic theologians would say) for the benefit of others who do struggle and suffer at the mercy of a kingdom of sin and death. It is not the case, for example, that Jesus overcomes mortality as the incarnation of the Word before he is crucified.[63] To the contrary, Jesus does not overcome temptation until he is tempted, does not overcome fear of death until he feels it, at which time this temptation and fear are assumed by the Word. Jesus does not heal death until the Word assumes death when Jesus dies; Jesus does not conquer sin until he assumes or bears the sin of others by suffering death at their hands, the ultimate human rejection of God's beneficence offered in his person.

Here is a solution to the common problem of integrating the incarnation with the rest of those aspects of Jesus' life and death deemed

[62] See Barth, *Church Dogmatics* I/2, 153: 'there must be no weakening or obscuring of the saving truth that the nature which God assumed in Christ is identical with our nature as we see it in the light of the Fall.' For the early church, see, for example, John of Damascus, 'Exposition of the Orthodox Faith,' Book 3, chapter 20; and Gregory of Nyssa, 'An Address on Religious Instruction,' 305: 'For how could our nature be restored if it was . . . not this sick creature of earth, which was united with the Divine? For a sick man cannot be healed unless the ailing part of him in particular receives the cure.'

[63] See Barth, *Church Dogmatics* IV/2, 140–1.

to be saving – particularly, with the crucifixion.[64] Here the saving power of the cross is a product of the incarnation, as its effects are actualized over time in and through Jesus' actual dying.[65] The cross saves, not as a vicarious punishment or an atoning sacrifice or satisfaction of God's honor or as a perfectly obedient act – all those accounts of the cross that have become problematic for contemporary persons, especially since the lessons of white feminist, womanist, and liberation theology.[66] The cross saves because in it sin and death have been assumed by the one, the Word, who cannot be conquered by them. Christ is victor here, following Gustaf Aulén's famous typology, but the underlying model is that of the incarnation itself.[67] Christ is no doubt obedient here but that is simply another effect of the same saving mechanism of incarnation. Jesus suffers death so that we need not – our death is suffered by him vicariously, he substitutes himself for us on the cross, takes our place. But this is, again, the effect of his saving us and not the very means or mechanism by which Jesus saves. The cross is a sacrifice but only in the same sense that Jesus' whole life is a sacrifice of love. Following Cyril of Alexandria, the sacrifice here is a sacrifice of incarnation.[68] That God, out of love and concern for us, would so humble Godself as to unite Godself with not just lowly humanity but humanity in the most dire straits – that is the sacrifice, made by God in Christ on our behalf, in death as over the course of Jesus' whole life. The sacrifice on the cross has nothing essentially to

[64] For the charge that this is a problem, see Pannenberg, *Jesus – God and Man*, 306. For the general solution, see the patristic reading of what Barth is up to in Thomas F. Torrance, *Karl Barth, Biblical and Evangelical Theologian* (Edinburgh: T&T Clark, 1990), 201, 203–5, 228–9, 230–1. Torrance emphasizes what I am pushing even more strongly here: that this view of the connection between incarnation and atonement disrupts 'external forensic and juridical' accounts of the atonement.

[65] See Cyril of Alexandria, *On the Unity of Christ*, 115, 126–32; and Gregory of Nyssa, 'An Address on Religious Instruction,' 304–7, 309–12. The resurrection of the dead Jesus is the natural consequence of the incarnation, of the fact that Jesus' humanity is united with the life-giving Word.

[66] See, for example, Delores Williams, 'Black Women's Surrogate Experience and the Christian Notion of Redemption,' in *After Patriarchy*, ed. P. Cooey, W. Eakin, and J. McDaniel (Maryknoll, New York: Orbis Books, 1990).

[67] Compare Gustaf Aulén, *Christus Victor*, trans. A. G. Hebert (London: SPCK, 1965).

[68] See, *On the Unity of Christ*, 58; this is *kenosis* understood as a form of abasement. See also the helpful analysis of Cyril's position on this score in Frances Young, 'Christological Ideas in the Greek Commentaries on the Epistle to the Hebrews,' *Journal of Theological Studies* 20, part 1 (April 1969): 154, 159.

do with a blood sacrifice for the expiation of sin; Jesus' death is the simple consequence of the life he led on behalf of others – his soteriological mission – in a sinful world; death (and the sin that brought it) cannot conquer that mission because of the relation enjoyed with God in Christ.[69]

Contrary to the usual complaint against Alexandrian Christologies, here the humanity of Jesus is not sidestepped in favor of the saving powers of the Word. Jesus saves in virtue of the divine power of the Word but the Word clearly could not save without being incarnate, without actually assuming the human. Jesus saves therefore *as* a human being – for example, in and through the fact that he goes to the cross and comes out alive. Salvation occurs *in* a human life; that life is not incidental to salvation's achievement. Salvation is extended to us, moreover, only as the effects of incarnation come to be realized in Jesus' own life. The perfected humanity of Jesus is the means of our salvation; we are saved as we are united with him, perfected and glorified, in faith and love.

The process of purifying and elevating the human as that process covers *each* aspect of Jesus' life and death involves a happy exchange of divine and human powers, a communication of properties, the interpenetration of human and divine, in and through Jesus' acts.[70] On the one side, the human is communicated to the Word in the incarnation itself as the Word takes on the human for God's own saving purposes, an active assumption that incorporates, we have said, an element of process in so far as what is assumed is in process. On the flipside – the incarnation's effects on the human – the divinity of the Word is communicated to the human in what the early church called

[69] For the general question of Christian re-workings of notions of sacrifice, especially in liturgical practice, see Gordon Lathrop, *Holy Things* (Minneapolis: Fortress Press, 1998), chapter 6.

[70] For a case of what is at issue, see the nice statement of Cyril of Alexandria, *On the Unity of Christ*, 132, concerning the resurrection: 'There is nothing astonishing here, for if it is true that fire has converse with materials which in their own natures are not hot, and yet renders them hot since it so abundantly introduces to them the inherent energy of its own power, then surely in an even greater degree the Word who is God can introduce the life-giving power and energy of his own self into his very own flesh.'

For more general accounts of the process, see Thomas Aquinas, *Summa Theologiae*, IIIa, Q. 19; and John of Damascus, 'Exposition of the Orthodox Faith,' Book 3, chapter 15.

Jesus' theanthropic operations. The gifts of the Word are communicated to, they suffuse, Jesus' humanity like fire through iron so as to purify, heal and elevate it, in a new form of living. Through such a process, the Word forms the character of Jesus' acts; the way that Jesus lives takes on the shape of the second Person of the Trinity. Such are the consequences for Jesus' humanity of the fact that his existence is the very existence of the Son:

> The particularity of Jesus Christ . . . and therefore of the determination of His human essence by the grace of God, emerges . . . when we look first to the origin of His being as the Son of man, of his human existence. . . . The grace of His particular origin consists in the fact that He exists as man . . . in the mode of existence of the Son [who is] God Himself. . . . It is not only because God exists that this One exists as man. The same is true of every man. . . . [I]t is true in particular of the Son of Man Jesus Christ that . . . He also exists as God exists. His existence as man is identical with the existence of God in His Son.[71]

As the consequences of this identity unroll over the course of Jesus' human life, what humanity and divinity are capable of come to interpenetrate in an active way, through a style of life that shows human inclinations in the process of being made over, made new, so as to produce a mode of existence that realizes on the human plane the mode of existence that defines the second Person of the Trinity.[72] A *locus classicus* of this process can be found in the words attributed to Jesus in the Garden of Gethsemane: 'Father, if it is possible let this cup pass from me; yet not my will but your will be done.' A human fear of death, both natural and accentuated by anxiety before death as what brings separation from God through sin to its awful culmination, is

---

[71] Barth, *Church Dogmatics* IV/2, 90.

[72] For this understanding of 'mode,' according to which the mode of existence of the divine *ousia* that is the second Person of the Trinity corresponds to the 'mode' or manner of Jesus' living, see Maximus the Confessor, 'Opuscule 3,' trans. Andrew Louth, in *Maximus the Confessor* (London and New York: Routledge, 1996), 194. See also J. P. Garrigues, 'La Personne composée du Christ d'après saint Maxime le Confesseur,' *Revue Thomiste* 74, no. 2 (April–June 1974): 199–204. And finally, Thomas Aquinas, *Summa Theologiae*, IIIa, Q. 2, A. 6, ad 1: 'the human nature of Christ is likened to . . . a garment . . . inasmuch as the Word is seen by the human nature, as a man by his garment, and . . . inasmuch as the garment is changed, for it is shaped according to the figure of him who puts it on;' and Q. 18, A.1, ad 4: 'Hence the human will of Christ had a determinate mode from the fact of being in a Divine Hypostasis, i.e., it was always moved in accordance with the bidding of the Divine will.'

here expressed, accompanied by the tears and tribulation that are the human lot under conditions of sin, and then overcome through conformity with the will of the Father, a conformity that is naturally Jesus' own in virtue of his being the Son of God, the one whose very will is the will of Father.[73]

Finally, the Christology I am offering here does not make Jesus' relation to the Word overshadow the scriptural emphasis given to Jesus' relations with the Father – a problem that many contemporary theologians think afflicts incarnational Christologies.[74] That no more happens than the incarnation overshadows its effects in perfected humanity – and for the same reason. Jesus does not have a relation to the Word comparable to the relations he enjoys with the Father, as scripture tells it. He enjoys a perfect fellowship with the Father but he is the Word. In imitation of Jesus' relations with the Father, Jesus does not reflect in some interior monologue on how to conform his human will to the Word's or his human knowledge to the Word's omniscience – we ruled out anything like this before when we discussed divine transcendence.[75] Jesus does the Word's will and reflects the Word's omniscience in his actions, simply because he is the Word. The human being Jesus in process of purification and elevation, the flipside and inseparable effect of incarnation, has a relationship with the Father – relations of love and prayerful trust and conformity of purpose and action – as a human manifestation of the relations enjoyed by the first and second Persons in the Trinity. In virtue of the incarnation, then – not as an alternative to it or replacement for it – Jesus relates to the Father, the first Person of the Trinity, in

---

[73] See John of Damascus, 'Exposition of the Orthodox Faith,' Book 3, chapter 18; and Maximus the Confessor, 'Opuscule 7,' trans. Andrew Louth, in *Maximus the Confessor* (London and New York: Routledge, 1996), 186–7. See also the fine discussion of Maximus the Confessor's treatment of this biblical passage in David Yeago, 'Jesus of Nazareth and Cosmic Redemption: The Relevance of St Maximus the Confessor,' *Modern Theology* 12, no. 2 (April 1996): 191 n. 39.

[74] For this charge, see, again, Pannenberg, *Jesus – God and Man*, 334.

[75] See Maximus, 'Opuscule 3,' 93–4. Jesus does not bring an independently active human will into line with the fact that he is the Word; the only acts of will that Jesus has are those shaped by the Word. See also John of Damascus, 'Exposition of the Orthodox Faith,' Book 3, chapter 14. There are not two acts of will – a human will and the Word's direction of it – to be co-ordinated (or possibly fall out of sync), but one complex one – a human will shaped by the Word.

the mode of existence of the Son, the second Person of the Trinity, made human.

I have emphasized in this chapter the soteriological point of the incarnation for human life and its human dimensions, but what might all this mean for us and for the ordinary affairs of life? The next chapter begins my approach to this question.

2

The Theological Structure
of Things

In the last chapter I highlighted how Jesus' human way of life in the world might be the point of a traditionally formulated, but significantly reconceived Chalcedonian Christology. In this chapter, I want to draw out the meaning of Christ's human way of life for us, by situating it within a very broad cosmo-theological frame. Where do humans fit in a broader theological scheme of things that has Christ as its center? With this as a basis, I proceed in the next chapter to a more concrete discussion of the shape of human life.

One comes to understand better theologically the meaning of human life by placing it within a whole structure of oddly similar but materially different gift-giving relations that bring together or unite God and the world. Human life takes on sense when it is positioned within 'a recurrent analogical "structure" of different types of union between God and what is not God.'[1] These different relations of connection or union elucidate one another, as they become visible in light of one another around a couple of organizing centers: the Trinity and the incarnation.

The triune God is a God who perfectly communicates the goodness of Godself among the three Persons of the Trinity in perfect self-unity. Expressing this dynamic life outward in a grace of beneficent love for what is not God, the triune God brings about a variety of different

---

[1] Henk Schoot, *Christ the 'Name' of God: Thomas Aquinas on Naming Christ* (Leuven: Peeters, 1993), 188.

forms of connection or union with the non-divine, for the sake of perfecting what is united with God, in an effort to repeat the perfection of God's own triune life. 'God, full beyond all fulness, brought creatures into being . . . so that they might participate in Him in proportion to their capacity and that He Himself might rejoice in His works . . . through seeing them joyful and ever filled to overflowing with His inexhaustible gifts.'[2] In a variety of distinct forms of connection or union in the gift-giving effort, God's work begins with creation, continues in historical fellowship with a particular people, Israel, and ends with Jesus as the one through whom, in the Spirit, all people and the whole world will show forth God's own triune goodness in unity with God. The incarnation is the perfect form of such relations of connection or union for gift-giving ends: 'it belongs to the essence of the highest good [that is, God] to communicate itself in the highest manner to the creature, and this is brought about chiefly by His so joining created nature to Himself that one Person is made up. . . . Hence, . . . it was fitting that God should become incarnate.'[3] In order for the whole of the human and natural worlds to be perfected with God's own gifts, they must be assimilated to this perfect relation between God and the created world in Christ, by way of him. Indeed, the Word, with the Spirit, sent by the Father, has, since the beginning of the world in diverse fashions, been working for the embodiment of God's goodness in it. By assuming human nature in all its embodied connectedness and embeddedness in its physical surroundings, the Word in Christ joins the human as well as the natural world with God.

> It is in the body that we stand in solidarity with the whole material creation. All this God has taken into himself, in sharing man's bodily condition of weakness and limitation: 'O marvellous device of divine wisdom and love, uniting things lowest with the highest, human with the divine, through our nature, the least and last and sunken lower still, raising up the whole universe into union with himself, encircling and enfolding all with his love, and knitting all in one; and that through us!'[4]

---

[2] Maximus the Confessor, 'Third Century of Love,' trans. G. Palmer, P. Sherrard, and K. Ware, in *The Philokalia*, vol. 2 (London: Faber & Faber, 1981), section 46.

[3] Thomas Aquinas, *Summa Theologiae*, trans. Dominican Fathers (Westminster, Maryland: Christian Classics, 1981), IIIa, Q. 1, A. 1, body.

[4] A. M. Allchin, *Participation in God* (Wilton, Connecticut: Morehouse-Barlow, 1988), 60, citing E. B. Pusey's *Sermons* (1845), 294.

Human beings who are one with Christ, by the Spirit, further the effort for all people and for the cosmos as a whole in recognition of their essential links with all others and their inextricable being in the midst of the natural world. Thus, 'we have always to remember that God's glory really consists in His self-giving, and that this has its centre and meaning in God's Son, Jesus Christ, and that the name of Jesus Christ stands for the event in which man, and in man the whole cosmos, is awakened and called and enabled to participate in the being of God.'[5] Through Christ, human beings have a crucial mediatorial role to play in God's gift-giving ends for one another and the whole world: 'In his way to union with God, man in no way leaves creatures aside, but gathers in his love the whole cosmos disordered by sin, that it may at last be transfigured by grace.'[6] God's whole effort to share God's trinitarian life with the world, with all its many distinct facets, is in this way focused in Christ: 'The incarnation of the Word of God at Bethlehem, in Galilee, in Jerusalem, is not an isolated wonder, but a central focal point in a network of divine initiatives which spread out into the whole of human history, indeed into the whole universe.'[7]

Situated within this theological structure of many different parallel or analogous relations of gift-giving unity, human life – indeed, any aspect of the structure (say, Christ himself on the account I offered in the last chapter) – gains a greater intelligibility, as each aspect becomes a kind of commentary on the others. Intelligibility here is like that of myth according to Claude Lévi-Strauss, where conundrums are naturalized, rather than resolved, by repeating them across a variety of domains.[8] Or it is like the intelligibility provided by a Freudian

---

[5] Karl Barth, *Church Dogmatics* II/1, trans. G. W. Bromiley and T. F. Torrance (Edinburgh: T&T Clark, 1957), 670.

[6] Vladimir Lossky, *The Mystical Theology of the Eastern Church* (Crestwood, New York: St Vladimir's Seminary Press, 1976), 111, discussing the views of Maximus the Confessor.

[7] A. M. Allchin, *Participation in God*, 72, discussing Maximus the Confessor. On this as the view of Bonaventure, see Ewert Cousins, *Bonaventure and the Coincidence of Opposites* (Chicago: Franciscan Herald Press, 1979), 206–7: 'although the coincidence of opposites is the universal logic of Bonaventure's system, each major area of his thought has its own specific form of the coincidence of opposites based on the metaphysical structure of that area. The notion of Christ the center, then, accounts for the common logic at the same time that it sustains the specific difference of each class.'

[8] See Claude Lévi-Strauss' treatment of myth in his *Structural Anthropology*, trans. C. Jacobson and B. Schoepf (New York: Basic Books, 1973).

recounting of the compulsive repetition of traumatic events in a person's life – though in the theological case what is recounted is good after good.[9] In such cases, meaning is enhanced as a similar structure variously permutated becomes visible.

The Trinity

Let us begin discussion of this theological structure with the triune God. There are, appropriately enough, three ways of talking about the perfect unity of the Trinity as a relation that implies the perfection of the three Persons. One can talk of this unity in terms of a unity of essence or substance; in terms of co-inherence of substance and Persons; and in terms of indivisibility in action: 'owing to their having the same essence and dwelling in one another, and being the same in will, and energy, and power, and authority, and movement, so to speak, we recognise . . . the unity of God.'[10]

Unity of essence or substance does not mean that the Persons of the Trinity are like one another in virtue of a shared generic nature – the way three people are like one another in that they are all human.[11] Unity of essence or substance means that the three Persons of the Trinity are the very same thing or concrete substance in three modes or forms of presentation.[12] They are like three distinct appearances of the same thing from different angles, although here such appearances are objective and lasting, unlike the transient effects of perspective, and although here the whole is presented differently and not just one side or part becoming visible from a particular point of view. The very same thing is therefore found repeated in Father, Son and Holy Spirit,

---

[9] Lévi-Strauss' interpretation of myth was influenced by Freud's talking cure, I believe.

[10] John of Damascus, 'Exposition of the Orthodox Faith,' trans. S. Salmond, *Nicene and Post-Nicene Fathers*, vol. 9 (Peabody, Massachusetts: Hendrickson Publishers, 1994), 10.

[11] Such is not the Cappadocian view, despite the often misinterpreted passage in Gregory Nazianzus, 'Fifth Theological Oration,' trans. C. Browne and J. Swallow, in *Christology of the Later Fathers*, ed. Edward Hardy (Philadelphia: Westminster Press, 1954), paragraph 11. The analogy with Seth and Eve (or elsewhere in the Cappadocians, Abel and Adam) has to do with the implications of their difference from one another – the one being begotten and the other not. The analogy is not meant to suggest that the essence of the Trinity is generic – the analogy does not hold in that respect – as is made clear in paragraphs 14 and 15.

[12] See G. L. Prestige, *God in Patristic Thought* (London: SPCK, 1952), 102–3, 157–9, 168, 173, 213–15, 229–30, 234–5.

although none of these Persons is to be identified with any other: the Father is all that the Son is except the Son is not the Father, etc.

The three therefore co-inhere, they are in one another, in virtue of this same essence or substance reappearing in them in different modes of existence. And one can also say, for the same reason, that the three are in one another personally: the Father is in the Son and the Son in the Father, etc. As Athanasius puts it: 'For the Son is in the Father . . . because the whole Being of the Son is proper to the Father's essence . . . so that whoever sees the Son, sees what is proper to the Father, and knows that the Son's Being, because from the Father, is therefore in the Father.'[13] Thus, the Son is the very will or heart of the Father, and that will or heart remains in the Father – the Father does not lose his own will or heart through its communication to the Son. Therefore the Son is in the Father (because the will or heart which is the Son remains with and in the Father) and the Father is in the Son (in that it is the very will or heart of the Father that is communicated to the Son, flowing out as the Son), and so on.

What the first Person of the Trinity is essentially is communicated totally or completely to the other two, without the loss or depletion of what the first is and remains. Their relationship in this respect is like that of source of light, ray of light and illumination.[14] On an equal footing with the Father, without any distance of space or interval of time, the Son and Spirit are, moreover, already essentially, what they are given from the Father – they are already by nature what they receive.[15] They have by rights of nature what they are given; what they are given is their very own.[16] The image here is of three perfectly overlapping suns, in an ordered mutual illumination: 'it is just like three suns cleaving to each other without separation and giving out light mingled and conjoined into one.'[17]

---

[13] Athanasius, 'Four Discourses against the Arians,' trans. J. H. Newman and A. Robertson, *Nicene and Post-Nicene Fathers*, vol. 4 (Grand Rapids: Eerdmans Publishing Company, 1957), discourse 3, section 3.

[14] Athanasius' favored imagery; see ibid., 313, 315, 364–6.

[15] See Hilary of Poitiers, 'On the Trinity,' trans. E. Watson and L. Pullan, *Nicene and Post-Nicene Fathers*, vol. 9 (Peabody, Massachusetts: Hendrickson Publishers, 1994), 65.

[16] Ibid., Book 6, section 27.

[17] John of Damascus, 'Exposition of the Orthodox Faith,' 11. See also Gregory of Nyssa, 'Against Eunomius,' trans. W. Moore and H. Wilson, *Nicene and Post-Nicene Fathers*, vol. 5 (Peabody, Massachusetts: Hendrickson Publishers, 1994), Book 1, section 36.

The three are united, finally, in an indivisible action together, both
in relation to one another as a living dynamism and in relation to the
world. Thus, the Father at once brings forth the Son out of himself –
like a beam of light that perfectly reflects its source. And from the
Father through the Son comes the Spirit – the illumination of that
beam, the beam's own illumination, the radiance in which it is seen
and which it projects. The Spirit proceeds from the Father to be with,
to rest in the Son, thereby suffusing the Son with the very effulgence
of the Father's own light that shines back to the Father from the
Son, carried along by the Spirit.[18] The Spirit bears and attests to the
loving union of Father and Son by bringing the Son's love for the
Father, the very love of the Father communicated from the Father to
the Son, back to the Father.[19] All at once this community of action is
the life of the triune God.

All at once, each making a distinctive contribution – Father as
source, Son as power or shape, Spirit as effecting, conveying and
completing – they also act as one *ad extra* in virtue of the single power
and operation that characterizes their self-same concrete substance or
essence.[20] From the Father, through the Son, in the Spirit, is the world
created, saved, and brought to its end or consummation. By the breath
of his mouth and in the image of his Word, the Father creates,
preserves and saves the world; the Father brings into being, orders,
and redeems, using, as Irenaeus would say, his two hands, Son and
Spirit.

In every case, the Father works, the Son works, the Spirit works –
all together, each in their distinct mode. But the working is not threefold in the way three human beings' working together would be, since
here, in virtue of their identity of substance or essence, the will to
work – in its exercise, particular shape, and general capabilities – is
the very same among the three. Among the Persons of the Trinity,

[18] See Dumitru Staniloae, *Theology and the Church*, trans. R. Barringer (Crestwood, New
York: St Vladimir's Seminary Press, 1980), 17, 18, 20, 25, 63.
[19] Ibid., 30, 32, 36.
[20] See Prestige, *God in Patristic Thought*, 256–8. For the way in which the three Persons of
the Trinity work all together as one without loss of their distinct contributions, see the excellent
discussion of Bruce Marshall, 'Action and Person: Do Palamas and Aquinas Agree about the
Spirit?' *St Vladimir's Theological Quarterly* 39, no. 4 (1995): 394–401.

since there is but one nature, there is also but one natural will. And again, since the subsistences [Persons] are unseparated, the three subsistences have also one object of will and one activity. In the case of men, however [no matter how similar their wills are as human beings] their acts of will and their opinions are different

and therefore are at best merely conjoined when working together.[21] As Athanasius says, it is fitting, for example, that the Word of God be Framer and Maker, that the Father create the world through the Word, 'since the Word is the Son of God by nature proper to his essence,' and therefore 'is the Father's will.'[22] Bernard succinctly states the basis for such a position:

> There is in them . . . one essence and one will, and where there is only one, there can be no agreement or combining or incorporation or anything of that kind. . . . [I]f anyone would affirm that there is agreement between the Father and the Son, I do not contest it provided that it is understood that there is not a unity of wills but a unity of will.[23]

Creation and Covenant

The free offer of this perfect fullness outward to what is not God finds its imperfect expression in the world as it is created, sustained, and directed generally by God. Existing through the outreach of the Holy Spirit, coming forth from the Father as the source of all good in the form of or after the image of the Father which is the Son, and pervaded as the Son is by the Spirit resting on and through it, the world as it comes to be and takes shape from God reflects the dynamics of the trinitarian life. The world does so, however, in a non-divine and therefore only approximate fashion. Unlike the trinitarian relations of perfect unity among the perfect, here in the triune God's relations to the world what God relates to cannot contain God, because it is not God; co-inherence is therefore not mutual, and the terms of the relation remain in some sense external to one another, at a distance.

[21] John of Damascus, 'Exposition of the Orthodox Faith,' 37.
[22] Athanasius, 'Four Discourses against the Arians,' 364–5. See also Gregory of Nyssa, 'Against Eunomius,' 72, 76, 81.
[23] Bernard of Clairvaux, On the Song of Songs, trans. I. Edmonds, vol. 4 (Kalamazoo, Michigan: Cistercian Publications, 1980), Sermon 71, section 9.

God cannot give Godself, in imitation of trinitarian relations of perfect divine communion, to what is not God, simply as such. Unlike the fully consubstantial Persons of the Trinity, creatures are not of the same essence or substance as God and therefore the Persons of the Trinity cannot communicate to creatures what they communicate to one another. The diffusion of God's goodness cannot be complete in any creature, simply as such, and so none can say with the Son 'all that the Father has is mine.'[24] Initially at least, then, 'the diffusion that occurred in time in the creation of the world is no more than a pivot or point in comparison with the immense sweep of the divine goodness.'[25]

God from the start is giving all God can but the creature from the start cannot receive it. Rather than giving God again, so to speak – the giving that characterizes the intra-trinitarian communication of goodness – God in creating and upholding the world in goodness gives the creature itself instead. From out of God's stores, God provides to the world its created, non-divine existence, and all that it includes: life, truth, beauty, goodness in their finite forms.

Creation as non-divine also cannot even receive at once all that God wants to give in this way. God's gifts come to it over the course of time in what God intends to be an unending expansion of its ability to receive created gifts from the Father's hands of Son and Spirit. In keeping with this understanding of the limitations of creaturely finitude, Irenaeus talks of the creature's growth into gifts of God in so far as it remains open or plastic to God's influence: Thus, 'man receives advancement and increase towards God. For as God is always the same, so also man, when found in God, shall always go on towards God. For neither does God at any time cease to confer benefits upon, and to enrich man; nor does man ever cease from receiving the benefits and being enriched by God.'[26] Out of the same recognition of creaturely finitude, Gregory of Nyssa puts forward his notion of *epectasis*, the

---

[24] Bonaventure, *Collations on the Six Days*, trans. J. de Vinck, in *The Works of Bonaventure*, vol. 5 (Patterson, New Jersey: St Anthony Guild Press, 1970), eleventh collation, section 11.

[25] Bonaventure, *Itinerarium Mentis ad Deum*, chapter 6, section 2, according to the translation of Cousins, *Bonaventure and the Coincidence of Opposites*, 105.

[26] Irenaeus, 'Against Heresies,' *Ante-Nicene Fathers*, vol. 1 (Edinburgh: T&T Clark, 1989), 474; see also 399, 427, 478, 496, and esp. 521–3.

creature's constant forward motion or journey beyond itself into the boundlessness of God's fullness as the creature's capacities are stretched by what it receives: 'participation in the divine good is such that . . . it makes the participant ever greater and more spacious than before. . . . [E]verything that flows in produces an increase in capacity.'[27]

God therefore permeates creation with the created versions, so to speak, of God's own goodness: '[W]hen one considers the universe, can anyone be so simple minded as not to believe that the Divine is present in everything, pervading, embracing and penetrating it? For all things depend on Him who is, and nothing can exist which does not have its being in Him who is.'[28] As the early church expressed the idea, God contains the world, in the sense of both supporting and pervading it with gifts from God's own store of trinitarian goodness. This relation, however, is not mutual, as it is for the Persons of the Trinity: the world does not and cannot contain or pervade God, the way the trinitarian Persons contain, envelop or are in one another.

> While present in the whole creation, [the Word] is at once distinct in being from the universe, and present in all things by his own power – giving order to all things, and over all and in all revealing his own providence, and giving life to each thing and all things, including the whole without being included, but being in his own Father alone wholly and in every respect.[29]

Because God is not finite as the world is, the world does not and cannot circumscribe, enclose, or fill up God with its good things, the way God does it.[30]

These gifts of God to the created world are external to or 'distant' from God, they are at a remove from God, in that they are non-

---

[27] Gregory of Nyssa, 'On the Soul and Resurrection,' PG 46.105B-C, trans. H. Musurillo, following J. Daniélou, quoted in Jean Daniélou's introduction to *From Glory to Glory: Texts from Gregory of Nyssa's Mystical Writings* (Crestwood, New York: St Vladimir's Seminary Press, 1995), 62–3. See Daniélou's introduction for a good description of *epectasis*, 56–71.

[28] Gregory of Nyssa, 'An Address on Religious Instruction,' trans. C. Richardson, in *Christology of the Later Fathers*, ed. Edward Hardy (Philadelphia: Westminster Press, 1954), 302.

[29] Athanasius, 'On the Incarnation of the Word,' trans. A. Robertson, in *Christology of the Later Fathers*, ed. Edward Hardy (Philadelphia: Westminster Press, 1954), 70–1.

[30] See Prestige, *God in Patristic Thought*, on the relations of container/contained, as they hold for God and creation, 27–36, and for the divine Persons, 284–90. See also John of Damascus, 'Exposition of the Orthodox Faith,' Book 1, chapters 13–14.

divine goods and not the communication of God's very own triune being.[31] But in a certain sense what is created is inseparable from God: without its continued sustenance from God's fountain of life, light, and goodness, the world would sink into nothingness. Unlike, however, the case of the Trinity, where the Persons are indivisible because they are as much themselves as the others, here the world's inseparability from God is a function of the world's deficiency. Creation depends on God for all the good things that it is, and is in that sense inseparable from God, just because it is not God.[32]

This inseparability, or relation of continued dependence between creatures and God, entails a form of correspondence in action between God and the world. To the extent that what happens in the world is good and for the good, the triune God is bringing those happenings to be in that way as their creator, preserver and director. This is, however, a kind of external correspondence; the creature's action is only its own, not also God's own, God's action simply matching it on some other vertical plane by which the creature's act is brought to be. Moreover, here where created happenings follow God's will for them, they do so unconsciously, without knowingly and willingly doing so; this is a blind following.[33] In both ways, God's acting with creatures who also act diverges from the model of trinitarian co-activity.

The triune God moves beyond this general level of created gifts by becoming the explicit object of active correspondence in the series of partnerships or fellowships between God and creatures discussed in the Old Testament, for example, those surrounding the faith and deeds of Adam and Eve, Noah, Abraham, and Moses, covenants of varying degrees of inclusivity, but all centering on this particular people, Israel,

---

[31] Gregory of Nyssa in 'Against Eunomius' emphasizes this fact; it is one way that relations between God, the Father, and the world are distinguished from the Father's relations with Son and Spirit; the latter are not separated by any temporal or ontological interval; see 165–6, 173.

[32] See, for example, Thomas Aquinas, Summa contra Gentiles, trans. C. O'Neil (Notre Dame, Indiana: University of Notre Dame Press, 1975), Book 4, chapter 8, section 9, where, against Arius, Aquinas is trying to show that the Son's inability to do anything without the Father is not like the case of creatures who cannot act without God because of their deficiency.

[33] See Bernard of Clairvaux, On Grace and Free Choice, trans. D. O'Donovan (Kalamazoo, Michigan: Cistercian Publications, 1977), 102–4: apart from further gifts of grace to the world, there are just material and biological beings who do the will of God without knowing it and some rational beings (wicked angels, sinful humans) who do the will of God while not wanting to.

in order, one might argue, to move out from there to the nations and the world as a whole. Here God communicates God's plenitude not just in created versions: here God is gift, Godself is what is given, as covenant partner.

> The work of His creation, and His control as the One who preserves and accompanies and rules the creature and therefore man, is certainly a favour out of His fullness. But in the covenant . . . He does not merely give out of His fulness. In His fulness He gives Himself to be with man and for man. As the benefit which He is in Himself, He makes Himself the companion of man.[34]

This stronger form of connection between God and creatures enables human beings to recognize and consciously to correspond in their own acts to God's will for the world. By way of human beings the world may no longer be simply a mute reflection of God's glory:

> [O]ut of his abundant love, [God] fashioned and created such a creature [with the capacity to reflect consciously on God's self-diffusive goodness in creation]. For it was not right that light should remain unseen, or glory unwitnessed, or goodness unenjoyed, or that any other aspect we observe of the divine nature should lie idle with no one to share or enjoy it.[35]

In human action, God as communicator of all good gifts might have a willing partner dedicated to God's own cause: ' "We are God's fellow workers (1 Cor. 3.9)" . . . as often as [God] deigns [to allow us] to perform some good act through him and with him . . . in that we have become united with the divine will by our own voluntary consent.'[36]

Unlike trinitarian relations, these covenant relations are still, however, relations at a distance. Human intentions must be brought into correspondence with the will of God in a kind of conference. With apologies to advocates of a social Trinity, the Persons of the Trinity do not confer with one another like this; they each have the will of the other.

> 'He spake and they were made'. . . . [N]ot that, as in the case of men, some under-worker might hear, and learning the will of Him who spoke might go away and do it; for this is what is proper to creatures, but it is unseemly so to

[34] Karl Barth, *Church Dogmatics* IV/1, trans. G. W. Bromiley and T. F. Torrance (Edinburgh: T&T Clark, 1956), 40.
[35] Gregory of Nyssa, 'An Address on Religious Instruction,' 276.
[36] Bernard, *On Grace and Free Choice*, 104.

think or speak of the Word. . . . For when that Word Himself works and creates, then there is no questioning and answer, for the Father is in Him and the Word in the Father.[37]

Because of the distance in relations between them, the gifts of conscious recognition and correspondence in action between human beings and God can be lost; these gifts prove temporary, fleeting achievements at best.[38]

> The word through which God communicated himself in the Old Testament was not a permanent conversation with himself in the prophet's heart of hearts, still less in the hearts of all men. . . . [M]en were not raised up to the level at which they could constantly listen and respond to the divine Word that was constantly being heard, or at least was always to be found among them. Consequently, man was not elevated to, nor did he operate within, the condition in which he himself was a permanent word immediately dependent on the divine Word. The dialogue was intermittent; the divine and human partners remained separated by a certain distance.[39]

Indeed, the same self-gift of God – in revelation and in laws for human behavior – that enables conscious recognition and the achievements of correspondence of will between God and humans also makes possible the deliberate failure of humans to reflect God's intentions for the world, the human refusal of God's hopes for the world as a place where God's perfect triune self-communication of goodness might be imitated. Human beings in this way sin, by closing their eyes to and blocking the reception of God's gifts to themselves and others.[40]

Jesus

In order to secure these gifts – in order to secure, indeed, all the gifts of God to creatures – God must relate to us in a less external way than God does in covenant relations with us.[41] This God does in Christ. The perfections of Jesus' humanity and the perfect fellowship Jesus

---

[37] Athanasius, 'Four Discourses against the Arians,' 365.

[38] Ibid., 415. See also John of Damascus, 'Exposition of the Orthodox Faith,' Book 4, chapter 4.

[39] Staniloae, *Theology and the Church*, 161.

[40] For this account of sin, see, for example, Gregory of Nyssa, 'An Address on Religious Instruction,' 280, 282.

[41] See Athanasius, 'Four Discourses against the Arians,' 385–6, 415.

THE THEOLOGICAL STRUCTURE OF THINGS

enjoys as a human being with the Father are not his as gifts (in a narrow sense), as they would be to an ordinary human partner in covenant with God. They are instead his by nature since here God becomes human; they come to his humanity not by some external grant but because God unites with humanity in Jesus, and thereby communicates goods to it.

Rather than simply communicate created goods, the triune God in the incarnation brings about what is other than God yet what is so united with God as to be God's own. Here is a genuine self-communication of God in the mode of the Son, without any distance between the Son and Jesus to be overcome or to provide the possibility of loss. Assumed by the second Person of the Trinity, in the hypostatic union discussed in the last chapter, the humanity of Jesus is both itself, the creature of God, and the very self-disclosure of the Father's good will for the world in the Son, the second Person of the Trinity.

Jesus' humanity is hypostasized or enhypostatic in the Son of God – Jesus exists as himself only as his humanity is assumed by the Son – in imitation of the way the Son (and the other members of the Trinity) are enhypostatic in the one triune life of God, or hypostatic in and by each other (the Son is itself – hypostatic – only in relation to the Father, that is, the Son is only the Son as the Son of the Father, and the reverse, and so on).[42] But here in the relation between Jesus and the Word there is only one *hypostasis*, not two – or three as in the Trinity. The human existence of Jesus is, then, the very mode of existence of the Son (and not some distinct one). Thereby Jesus enjoys the same relations with the Father and Spirit as the second Person of the Trinity does.

Unlike the unity of Persons in the Trinity by way of (*a*) unity of essence, (*b*) co-inherence and (*c*) indivisible action in three distinct and permanent modes, the humanity of Jesus is one with the Son of God by way of this very unity of *hypostasis*: The same one is both divine and human in virtue of the second Person of the Trinity's assumption of the humanity of Jesus. Human and divine functions remain distinct in Christ's life, nothing like the unity of substance or

---

[42] See Thomas F. Torrance, *The Trinitarian Faith* (Edinburgh: T&T Clark, 1988), 221, 226, 327.

nature found in the Trinity, though they have an identity of shape. Unlike the case of the Trinity, here co-inherence of functions and indivisibility of action follow from unity on the level of *hypostasis*, rather than the reverse: because the humanity of Jesus exists in the very mode of the second Person of the Trinity, Jesus' acts have a unity of operation and purpose despite the diversity of human and divine functions displayed in them.[43]

The assumption of humanity by the Son produces a co-inherence of divinity and humanity that better imitates the co-inherence enjoyed by members of the Trinity than does God's containing and pervading creation generally. With the so-called communication of idioms in Christ, the way God contains and pervades creation is deepened and the relation becomes more mutual without jeopardizing the inequality between them.[44] Humanity is in the Son or second Person of the Trinity, communicated to it, in that the Son assumes it as its own proper instrument for the distribution of benefits to the world. Without gaining anything itself through this communication of humanity to it – this is one way the relation of co-inherence is not mutual if God remains God – the Son shares in the operations of the humanity of Christ as that humanity is moved for saving ends according to God's free purposes. And because of that assumption by the Son, divinity is in or communicated to the humanity of Christ. Humanity's being in the Son has as its immediate effect the Son's being in the humanity of Christ – the priority of the former is another mark of non-mutuality appropriate to the difference between humanity and God. Divinity is communicated to humanity in that divinity provides the power by which humanity is (1) purified and securely perfected in its humanity, (2) elevated beyond its own created qualities – to immortality – and (3) given effects beyond what human beings are capable of (saving effects). In short, Jesus' humanity shares in divinity in the sense that particular characteristics and effects of its operations are supplied by God. It shares in divinity, moreover, not simply as moved by God –

---

[43] See John of Damascus, 'Exposition of the Orthodox Faith,' Book 3, chapters 15 and 19; also Karl Barth, *Church Dogmatics* IV/2, trans. G. W. Bromiley and T. F. Torrance (Edinburgh: T&T Clark, 1958), 114–16.

[44] For the following account of the communication of idioms, see Thomas Aquinas, *Summa Theologiae*, IIIa, Q. 19, A. 1.

like a naturally immobile axe might be swung by a bench maker and thereby share dumbly in the bench maker's purposes. It shares in the operations of God as it moves according to its own natural operations – like fire might be used by a smithy to heat iron. In other words, the operations proper to Jesus' humanity are the very ones in which God saves.

As a living display of this indwelling of divinity in humanity that follows from the assumption, divinity and humanity are united in Jesus' acts. They are clearly not united in act as the members of the Trinity are in virtue of an identity of nature. The acts of Jesus are not divine and human at once because the operations proper to humanity and divinity are identical. The acts of Jesus are, instead, genuinely two-fold in character, displaying both divinity and humanity as distinct features of the very same acts. Jesus' acts are one though twofold – not sometimes divine and sometimes human – and show a consistency of purpose and effect, because they are directed and shaped by the same one who is both divine and human, because in him human functions take on the divine shape or mode of Sonship.[45]

If human and divine are not united in the acts of Jesus with the sort of substantial or essential unity in action achieved by members of the Trinity, neither do the acts of Jesus unite humanity with divinity simply in the way the acts of creatures everywhere do: the purely human plane of action being held up into existence over its course by the power of God's creative will, from which it is inseparable. No, once, again, Jesus' acts are genuinely twofold in and of themselves, and that signals a level of unity between divinity and humanity in act greater here than elsewhere.

A greater level of unity is achieved here because, as we have said, the human character of these acts is God's own: Jesus' acts are not just God's own in virtue of the divine powers and functions they display; their human features are also God's own in virtue of their assumption by the Son of God. But, moreover, a greater level of unity between human and divine is achieved here because the powers of God are humanity's own – in two senses. First, in the sense that Jesus' humanity itself achieves human perfections, for example, sinlessness, in a

<hr>

[45] See n. 43 above.

complete and secure form that only divine power enables. These perfections, empowered as they are by God, are humanity's own in that they become characteristic of Jesus' humanity in and of itself – its own empirical or metaphysical attributes. A second set of perfections is, however, Jesus' humanity's own only in a weaker sense. When Jesus' humanity receives what is beyond human capacities – say, immortality – and is given the grace of participating in the very saving works of God, bringing about thereby what only God can bring about for others, this set of gifts does not, indeed cannot, become the properties of Jesus' humanity *per se*. These gifts are therefore not evident in created versions of divine qualities and powers – there are no created versions of these powers and qualities. This second set of gifts is Jesus' humanity's own only in relation to divinity; they are attributable to the human works of Jesus only in so far as Jesus' works are united to the Word through the Word's assumption of his humanity.[46]

Besides being in these ways a higher form of unity with God than creation generally enjoys, the incarnation is a higher form of unity than fellowship with God, and thereby the closest approximation to the triune life that is possible for a creature.[47] Here there is no externality between the human life of Jesus and the Word; Jesus does not enjoy fellowship with the Word; Jesus simply is the Word incarnate. The human will of Jesus does not conform itself to the Word as God's own will by way of deliberation; from the first it is nothing other than the will of the Son in the very shape or mode that distinguishes the Son from Father and Spirit in their dynamic interactions.[48]

Here, the relation between God and humanity does not simply imitate the triune life of God, because, here, that very triune life

---

[46] See John of Damascus, 'Exposition of the Orthodox Faith,' Book 3, chapters 17–18.

[47] I am disagreeing here with Karl Barth, who, to my mind, often assimilates the incarnation itself and the communication of idioms, which establishes the character of Jesus' person and acts in and of themselves, too closely to the idea of covenant or fellowship – for example, by using the categories of confrontation and address to talk about them. See Barth, *Church Dogmatics* IV/2, 84–8. The man Jesus who is the Word incarnate does (as we see below) exhibit a perfect human form of fellowship with Father and Spirit, but that is a logically distinct matter.

[48] See Maximus the Confessor, 'Difficulty 5,' 'Oposcule 7,' and 'Oposcule 3,' trans. A. Louth, in Andrew Louth, *Maximus the Confessor* (London and New York: Routledge, 1996), 171–97.

assumes humanity to itself. The result is the triune life in a human form: the Word becomes incarnate from the first, in Jesus' birth, through the inspiration of the Holy Spirit, as sent by the Father.[49] The man Jesus over the course of his life is, consequently, the Son of God following the will of the Father through the power of the Spirit, in order to distribute the goods of God to the world – healing, forgiving, directing the course of human lives in imitation of his own.[50] Whatever Jesus does for us, he does as the Word incarnate sent by God the Father through the power of the Spirit.

The humanity of Jesus himself is the first beneficiary of the new relation of humanity to divinity that is the incarnation: 'as Word, He gives from the Father, for all things which the Father does and gives, He does and supplies through Him; and as the Son of Man, He Himself is said after the manner of men to receive what proceeds from Him, because His Body is none other than His, and is a natural recipient of grace.'[51] Assumed by the Word, Jesus' humanity receives everything for its good directly from the source of goodness that is the Father through the power of the Spirit. This human being as the Word is the one whom God the Father favors with gifts through the working of the Holy Spirit – at Jesus' baptism, over the course of his struggles, and on the cross.

Favored with these gifts, Jesus in working for our salvation exhibits a perfect form of human partnership with the Father and Spirit, a human version of the Son's own action in common with the other members of the Trinity. As a human mode of the Son's own relations to Father and Spirit, this is covenant fellowship with God raised to a level otherwise impossible for creatures: this covenant fellowship *is* the indivisible co-action of the members of the Trinity.[52]

But it is the life of the Trinity extending its gifts to us with decisive differences that reflect the assumption of the human into it. Trinitarian relations, in other words, take on here the characteristics of fellowship or partnership just to the extent the Word takes humanity to itself in

[49] See Boris Bobrinskoy, *The Mystery of the Trinity*, trans. A. Gythiel (Crestwood, New York: St Vladimir's Seminary Press, 1999), 86–8.

[50] Ibid., 88–93.

[51] Athanasius, 'Four Discourses against the Arians,' 333.

[52] See Karl Barth, *Church Dogmatics* IV/3, trans. G. W. Bromiley and T. F. Torrance (Edinburgh: T&T Clark, 1962), 235–6.

Jesus.[53] Unlike trinitarian relations, the relation between the Word incarnate and the Father is an external one in some sense, a matter of fellowship rather than immediate unity of wills and operations, and a relation between subordinate and superior partners that reflects the difference between the humanity of Jesus and the divinity of the Father.[54] Or, at least these are the characteristics the relationship displays over the course of the historical and conflictual process by which Jesus' humanity is perfected. As his humanity is perfected through its assumption by the second Person of the Trinity, over the course of the conflict between inflowing gifts of grace from the Father and the circumstances of sin that affect the humanity of Jesus, Jesus prays to the Father, invokes the Father's help, acts in subordination to the Father. Because of the difference that the humanity of Jesus makes for the expression of the Trinity in Jesus' life, such acts of Jesus are a suitable model for us; Jesus in these ways becomes our companion in relations with the Father, through the power of the Spirit.

The final glorification of Jesus' humanity as that humanity eventually becomes perfect, through what Jesus both does and suffers, brings about a new stage of relationship, closer to the usual indivisibility of the Trinity apart from the assumption of the human. Glorified, Jesus' will would simply be that of the Father, Son and Spirit as one together, in their indivisible identity of will, and without becoming so, without any movement of collaborative fellowship by which one will is conformed to another. The humanity of Jesus *per se* might continue to grow in perfection, to expand to receive the gifts of God, but perhaps without a process of reception – no gradual growth into each one – and certainly without any struggle any longer against forces of sin and death.[55]

---

[53] See Athanasius, 'Four Discourses against the Arians,' 375–6, 380, 381; Hilary of Poitiers, 'On the Trinity,' 207; and Claude Welch, *In This Name* (New York: Charles Scribner's Sons, 1952), 264.

[54] Thus, Karl Barth draws too close a parallel between the relationship of Son and Father and the obedience and humility of the Word *incarnate* before the Father: see, for example, *Church Dogmatics* IV/1, 203–4; and IV/2, 343–4. Without making the work of the triune God *ad extra* at all foreign to the triune God's own dynamic life (which is Barth's fear), patristic writers make a salutary distinction here because of their fear of Arianism – that is, in order to avoid suggesting that the Son is subordinate to and less than the Father.

[55] What I am getting at here is obviously a patristic motif but see also the intimations of Barth about Christ the Redeemer in his *Ethics*, trans. G. W. Bromiley (Edinburgh: T&T Clark, 1981), 468, 469; the volumes of the *Church Dogmatics* that were to concern redemption (in distinction from reconciliation) were, aside from lecture fragments, never written.

Humanity

Once perfected by the inpouring of gifts from the Father, Jesus' humanity becomes the means by which those gifts are poured out to us through the workings of the Holy Spirit. So Athanasius says: 'As man, is He said to take what, as God, He ever had, that even such a grant of grace might reach to us.' 'The gifts which come from God . . . doth He too Himself receive, that man, being united to Him may be able to partake of them. Hence it is that the Lord says, "All things whatsoever Thou hast given Me, I have given them." '[56] And Calvin:

> 'He was anointed above his fellows' [Ps 45:7], for if such excellence were not in him, all of us would be needy and hungry. . . . [H]e did not enrich himself for his own sake, but that he might pour out his abundance upon the hungry and the thirsty. The Father is said 'not by measure to have given the Spirit to his Son' [John 3:34]. The reason is expressed as follows: 'That from his fullness we might all receive grace upon grace' [John 1:16]. From this fountain flows that abundance of which Paul speaks: 'Grace was given to each believer according to the measure of Christ's gift' [Eph. 4:7].[57]

Repeating with us what happens in the dynamic life of the Trinity apart from us, the Spirit proceeds from the Father to rest on Jesus, the Word incarnate. The Spirit radiates the humanity of Jesus with the Father's own gifts of light, life and love; and shines through him, not simply back to the Father, but through his humanity to us, thereby communicating to us the gifts received by Jesus from the Father.[58] In this way, the gifts of the Father indwell us in and through the gift of the Spirit itself shining through the glorified humanity of the Son. Thereby the Spirit in us effects created gifts in and for our humanity.

The condition for this inclusion of us in the dynamic of the Trinity's own life is our unity with Christ, which is also worked by the Holy Spirit as the Spirit of Christ, the Son, sent by him for the completion of the Father's work *ad extra*. It is as we are united to Christ by the Holy Spirit that we receive the perfections that Jesus received in his

---

[56] Athanasius, 'Four Discourses against the Arians,' 330, 435; see also, 331, 333–5.

[57] John Calvin, *Institutes of the Christian Religion*, ed. J. McNeil, trans. F. Battles, vol. 1 (Philadelphia: Westminster Press, 1960), Book 2, chapter 15, section 5, 499–500; see also, 528: 'since rich store of every kind of good abounds in him, let us drink our fill from his fountain.'

[58] See Staniloae, *Theology and the Church*, 199.

humanity.[59] United with Christ by the Holy Spirit we go with Christ to the Father, from whom we receive, as the humanity of Christ did, gifts from the Father.[60]

The communication to us of the perfections of Jesus' humanity takes this trinitarian shape, because Jesus' humanity saves in virtue of its being in the mode of the second Person of the Trinity. It is the particularity of Jesus' humanity, its specific shape or mode, that comes to include us. We are not included in Christ's life simply because the humanity assumed by the Son in Christ is common, shared by Christ and every other human being. It is this particular person – and not the humanity of Christ *per se* – that has universal efficacy, in so far as everyone else is drawn to it, united with Christ's own life. Jesus' own life, in its particular shape as a human version of the Son's, includes us by continuing in the form of a life with us, a life, that is, in which we are made to participate by the Holy Spirit. By embracing and integrating the lives of everyone else within itself, the life of Jesus generates histories with a form like itself.[61]

Christ can so draw everyone (once again) not so much because the humanity assumed in Christ is common to both Christ and us, but because the second Person of the Trinity is the one who assumes it.[62] The universal range of the incarnation's effects follows from the universal range of all the Son's workings *ad extra*, whereby the Son images the Father outward in the world as a whole, after its own image. What the Son did in the life that Jesus led was for the sake of all of us

[59] See Calvin, *Institutes of the Christian Religion*, Book 3, chapter 1, section 3, 541.

[60] On the first part of this statement – reflecting the patristic formula 'in the Spirit, through Christ, to the Father' – see Thomas F. Torrance, 'The Mind of Christ in Worship: The Problem of Apollinarianism in the Liturgy,' in his *Theology in Reconciliation* (Grand Rapids, Michigan: William B. Eerdmans, 1975), 139–214. *Pace* Torrance, however, the soteriological point of this first formula would seem to be, as Athanasius recognized, what is mentioned in the second part of my statement – gifts received thereby from the Father, according to the formula 'from the Father through the Son in the Spirit.' See Athanasius, 'Four Discourses against the Arians,' 330–1, 333–5, esp. 435.

[61] See John Webster, *Barth's Ethics of Reconciliation* (Cambridge: Cambridge University Press, 1995), 138, 71, 93, 225. See also Barth, *Church Dogmatics* IV/3, 182–3; and his *The Christian Life*, trans. G. W. Bromiley (Grand Rapids, Michigan: William B. Eerdmans, 1981), 19–21, 74.

[62] See Torrance, *Trinitarian Faith*, 155, 182–3, discussing Athanasius. See also Thomas Aquinas, *Summa Theologiae*, IIIa, Q. 4, A. 4, ad 1: Christ is able to save all because of the universal efficacy of this particular person as cause, not because of anything generic or common about his human nature.

and therefore in his life all our lives are enclosed and anticipated in their purified, healed and elevated mode.[63]

Since we are not the incarnate Word as Jesus is, we have gifts from the Father as gifts, by grace, and not by nature, as Jesus has them: 'Since Christ is God . . . "the fullness of the Godhead dwells bodily in Him in a manner that is according to essence" (Col. 2:9). The fulness of the Godhead dwells in us by grace when we gather into ourselves . . . virtue and wisdom.'[64] We are not the Word of God as Christ was; we are not one with the Word but only one with Christ, and that only through the gift of the Holy Spirit.

Therefore our acts are not saving as Jesus' are. Jesus' humanity is the one united with the Word that assumes it for our salvation; we are the ones saved through this act of God. Our graced lives are part of the effects of the incarnation which are universal in scope. The incarnation is achieved by Christ before Christ assumes us to himself; we are *all already* saved by Christ, in the sense that the saving power of Christ is already complete and does not need repeating or reenactment by any of us.

Breaking any perfect parallel too with the assumption of Jesus' humanity by the Word, we are united with Christ after the fact of our existence as a kind of second creation, a second birth or adoption to be the Son of God's own in Christ, to be children of the Father as Christ was the Father's own Son. In short, our humanity is not assumed by Christ, as Christ's was by the Word; our already formed persons are.

Because it occurs after the fact of our existence with an already established character, this union with Christ requires tending in a way that humanity's assumption by the Son of God in Christ did not. Our union with Christ must be nurtured through the workings of the Spirit.[65] Baptized, for example, into Christ, a struggle to shore up our oneness with him ensues; the character and quality of our union with

---

[63] See Barth, *Christian Life*, 74.

[64] Maximus the Confessor, 'Second Century on Theology,' trans. G. Palmer, P. Sherrard and K. Ware, in *The Philokalia*, vol. 2 (London: Faber & Faber, 1981), section 21.

[65] See, for example, Martin Luther, *Lectures on Galatians* (1535) in *Luther's Works*, vol. 26 (Saint Louis, Missouri: Concordia, 1963), 393, on growth in faith. See also G. Berkouwer, *Faith and Sanctification* (Grand Rapids, Michigan: William B. Eerdmans, 1952), 106, 130: growth in faith means that we come to rely more and more on God's grace.

Christ must be bettered, heightened from weak union to strong, for example, through the repeated performance of the Eucharist in the power of the Spirit.

Coming after the fact as it does, our assumption by Christ through the working of the Holy Spirit means Christ's assumption of us in our active sinfulness. When we are taken with Christ to the Father to be blessed as Christ's humanity was by the Father, we are also, then, being forgiven our sins; the Father's favor takes the form of mercy in our case. The Father favors us and showers us with gifts, not because we are not sinful but because we are seen in Christ, the one in whom we live, as those who are in need of the Father's help, through the Son, in the Spirit.

Sinners assumed by Christ, our living out of that assumption will be marked by great struggle, against our own sins as well as those of others.[66] The struggle for purification and perfection of our humanity will be more extensive and protracted than anything seen in Jesus. Rather than simple struggle against temptation and the sort of external conflicts that Jesus fought with the consequences of the sins of others meeting up with him from without, the struggle to purify and perfect our humanity will entail (in addition to all this) renewed conflicts with active sin in our very persons.

Christian lives reproduce in their own distinct way, then, the incarnation of Christ and its processional, conflictual effects over the course of a fully human life. They will also reproduce in their way Jesus' final post-resurrection perfection.

Christ's incarnation is matched by our assumption into Christ. Assumed by Christ, Christ becomes the subject of our acts in much the way the second Person of the Trinity is the subject of Jesus' acts.[67] Our acts are Christ's acts, we can say Christ acts when we act, in so far as what we are and do comes by way of the power of Christ, in

---

[66] See Gregory of Nyssa, 'An Address on Religious Instruction,' 303–4.

[67] See Wilfried Joest, *Ontologie der Person bei Luther* (Göttingen: Vandenhoeck and Ruprecht, 1967), 233–320; Ingolf Dalferth and Eberhard Jüngel, 'Person und Gottebenbildlichkeit,' *Christlicher Glaube in moderner Gesellschaft* , vol. 24 of *Enzyklopädische Bibliothek*, ed. F. Böckle, F.-X. Kaufman, et al. (Freiburg: Herder, 1981), 61–99; and Karl Barth, *Church Dogmatics* II/1, 149, 159–62; I/2, trans. G. Thomson and H. Knight (Edinburgh: T&T Clark, 1956), 313–14; and II/2, trans. G. W. Bromiley and T. F. Torrance (Edinburgh: T&T Clark, 1957), 539.

so far as we are carried beyond our capacities by Christ who takes us to himself. Being and doing what we can only be and do with him, our characteristics and achievements as graced persons are attributed to Christ.

Christ is the subject of our acts for the same reason the Son of God was the subject of Jesus' acts: because Christ's agency is primary in our graced lives the way the Word is primary in Jesus' life; we act in a purified, elevated fashion (to the extent that we do!) only because Christ first acts for us by assuming us to himself, through the power of the Spirit.

Despite the primacy of the Word as subject, in Jesus the same acts are attributed indifferently to either the human being Jesus or the Word incarnate; they are both Jesus' and the Word's because here the two are really one. Assumed by Christ, our graced lives, however, are more Christ's than ours. The character of our graced lives is alien to us as sinners. Unlike what happened in Jesus, we are not constituted from the first as subjects by such gifts; they come to us as already constituted persons in opposition to who we already are. Indeed, what we are and do as graced persons cannot be attributed to us at all, if 'us' means the people who are assumed by Christ. These characteristics and deeds are ours only in so far as we becomes ourselves – new people – in relation to Christ, assumed by him. We become new subjects of attribution as we become the predicates of Christ, as our lives, in other words, belong to him; only as subjects in that sense are graced characteristics as much our own as Christ's.

There are two subjects here, where a human being is assumed by Christ, and not one, as when the Son of God assumed humanity rather than a man. This difference means that, unlike Christ who simply is the Word, we come to Christ from a distance, by way of an external call; addressing us, Christ appears outside us as the one to whom we are to be united.[68] Our relation to Christ has more the flavor, then, of Christ's own relation to the Father, a relationship of fellowship and correspondence of wills. Our will is not Christ's will in the way the human will of Christ simply is the will of the Son, without needing to

---

[68] See Karl Barth, *Church Dogmatics* III/2, trans. G. W. Bromiley and T. F. Torrance (Edinburgh: T&T Clark, 1960), 164, 175.

be brought into correspondence with it. Instead, our lives are made over as a result of their being assumed.

Though Christ comes to us from outside us, Christ nevertheless becomes our own. Assumed by Christ, Christ lives in us, just as, assumed by the Son, Christ's human life showed the workings of the Word in and through it. Within our own lives, Christ works to revise the lives we would otherwise live without him. The force of our assumption by Christ is felt, as it was in Jesus' own life, in and through the way our lives are led, in and through what happens in them, the shape they take, whereby the gifts of God come to be distributed to us and through us to others – other persons and the world as a whole.

The one process – Christ's dwelling in us and the effects that has – is dependent upon the other – our being assumed into Christ's own life – though (again as they were in Christ) not in a temporal sequence. Because we have been assumed into Christ's life, the changes in our lives are continuously fed by the workings of Christ in us through the power of the Spirit. The two processes, moreover, do not simply run alongside each other; the one – assumption by Christ – is, instead, the immanent motor of the other. The character of graced lives is twofold or theanthropic in the way the acts of Christ's life were; graced acts seem made up of two different powers – our own and Christ's – Christ's accounting for any purifying, healing and elevating of our own capacities manifest in our acts.

In us, however, unlike the life of Christ, the two processes fall far short of any perfect correspondence of identity. In Christ, what the Father gives to the humanity of Jesus through the Son's assumption of it is identical with what Jesus gives back to the Father in and through a human life of praise and service. This is one continuous action, displaying the very same character throughout: God's love for human beings is the very love that this human being, Jesus, displays for those human beings and the very love that this human being, Jesus, reflects back to God. As Karl Barth expresses this equivalence: 'The self-giving in which God himself . . . became and is . . . this man, is that which is achieved and manifested in his self-giving to God as a human act.'[69] With us, there are two processes and they do not correspond at all

---

[69] See Barth, *Christian Life*, 75.

well, at least at first. What Christ gives us by assuming us is not simply identical with the lives we live because we live before being assumed by Christ; our lives must be made to conform to what Christ is giving. Our lives do not conform to what Christ is giving us and have to be brought into greater conformity with Christ's own action over time, because we are assumed by Christ as sinners.

> [I]n distinction from the angels of God and the company of men made perfect, [the church] finds in itself, both as a whole and in all its members, certain limits, not in the divine self-giving but in its own knowledge, its own freedom, and the form in which it may respond . . . . – a provisional form in contrast to the perfect form for which we may here and now wait, and to which the Church may move.[70]

The perfect correspondence of identity that is Christ's life remains our hope. Already achieved by Christ, who as the very same one is both the Son giving and the human being receiving, we aim towards this unity or identity by efforts, never completed in this life, to eradicate sin and match the life intended for us by Christ's assumption of us. Not simply a future yet to be for us and not simply the past achieved by Christ but not by ourselves, our future is present in us as Christ shapes us in accordance with himself.[71]

Corresponding to Christ's own resurrected life, some final glorification awaits us, then, in which the perfections of God's own life and light will be perfectly reflected back to God in us, the struggle against sin will be no more and we will hear the call of the Word, as Karl Barth suggests in his *Ethics*, as our very own voice.[72] The will of God for the communication of God's perfect fullness will no longer be heard as an external command obligating our service but as the natural inclination of our own hearts and minds.[73] Through our own witness and working as ministers of God's grace, the whole world will reflect God's glory in conscious praise. A kingdom or arena suffused by the very life of the Trinity will be all and all without struggle against a kingdom of moral and physical corruption and structures of injustice; the whole world will be victorious over sin and death as Christ was before us.

[70] Barth, *Church Dogmatics* II/1, 675.
[71] See Barth, *Church Dogmatics* IV/1, 116.
[72] Barth, *Ethics*, 480, 487, 492, 494, 501, 502–3, 505, 512, 514.
[73] Ibid., 498, 503.

More concretely stated, the two aspects of Christian life short of the eschaton – assumption by Christ and the working out of that in our lives – correspond to faith and works, to justification and sanctification, and to worship and discipleship, respectively. By all the former, through the power of the Holy Spirit we are united with Christ: in the justifying faith that adheres or cleaves to Christ, in hearing the gospel as an irrevocable summons to a transformed life, in being baptized, in being lifted up in the Eucharist to Christ in order to go with him to the Father, in making Christ the center or axis of all we are and do with the Spirit's help. In such ways Christ, in and through his own Spirit, makes us his own. In such extrospective movements of faith, praise, prayer and worship, empowered by the Spirit, the whole of our being is turned towards Christ and through Christ to the Father. Christ becomes the axis or center of our existence and in this way our lives are united with his.[74]

Through this union with Christ, gifts from the Father flow to us. The Eucharist is the visible manifestation of this. What happens throughout the course of our graced existence is made visible here as we are fed by the Father's food in and through Jesus' own body and blood, made ours by the Spirit. In the Eucharist we see the stuff of life being united with Christ through the power of the Spirit, in order to return to us from the Father in the new life-giving form of Jesus' own body and blood.[75] In the Eucharist we offer up the things of the earth for the Father's blessings through Christ, so that they become new for our renewed sustenance; we are empowered to do so in and with Christ who has already taken up the things of the earth by assuming our body in all its fragile connections with the natural world.

Eaten by us, made our own indeed in all the ways I mentioned, Jesus then indwells us by his Spirit, as the form of our own lives, in an extension of the way the second Person of the Trinity informed and shaped Jesus' own way of life. As Jesus' own, assumed by him, we are enabled through the gift of the Spirit to work as Jesus did, for the

---

[74] See Barth, *Church Dogmatics* IV/2, 560, 565, 576, on conversion's establishing the new axis around which one revolves.

[75] See John Zizioulas, *Being as Communion* (Crestwood, New York: St Vladimir's Seminary Press, 1985), 160; this is an Irenaean theme, as he notes. Zizioulas' stress, however, on human agency is worrisome; see 119.

communication of God's gifts to ourselves and others, in a struggle against sin in ourselves and others, the sins that impede such communication. Indwelling us, becoming ours, because we have become Christ's, the Spirit of Christ communicates the gifts of divinity to our humanity, in much the same way the Word communicated them to Jesus' own humanity, through the Spirit of anointing. Our humanity is thereby cleansed and perfected and shares in the distribution of the same goods of God to other people and the world. Feeling the effects of a communication of divinity to humanity like that found in Jesus' own life, we, in short, are sanctified and serve the ends of trinitarian love. Human beings become in this way the administrative center of cosmic-wide service.[76]

Although acts of praise and worship, on the one side, are distinguishable from acts of service on the other – the former, the way Christ assumes us; the latter, the way this assumption works itself out in our lives – the two are found mixed up together in fact. They are no more separable here than assumption and its effects were in the case of Christ. The acts by which we are assumed by Christ are not meeting their purpose unless they are part of a transformed life. And those works do not simply follow after that assumption, say, by way of faith as faith's temporal successors. Works do not so much issue from faith as a psychological state preceding and impelling them, as much as they issue continually from the overflowing of Christ's virtues to us, as those virtues become ours in faith.[77] Works, moreover, achieve their goodness, they become what they are, only as they are so empowered in and through assumption by Christ.[78] A life of service to God's ends becomes itself a form of worship and praise; it has its own extrospective, God-ward character, in recognition of its empowerment by the grace of God in Christ.

[76] See Paul Santmire, *The Travail of Nature* (Minneapolis: Fortress Press, 1985), 42, discussing the 'administrative anthropocentrism' of Irenaeus.

[77] See Barth, *Church Dogmatics* IV/2, 503–11, where participation in Christ is discussed as the motor of Christian lives; Berkouwer, *Faith and Sanctification*, 27–8, 52, 64, 74, 78; Brian Gerrish, *Grace and Gratitude* (Minneapolis: Fortress Press, 1993), 71–6, discussing Calvin; and Erwin Iserloh, 'Luther's Christ Mysticism,' in *Catholic Scholars Dialogue with Luther*, ed. Jared Wicks (Chicago: Loyola University Press, 1970), 45–58.

[78] See John Webster, *Barth's Moral Theology* (Grand Rapids, Michigan: William B. Eerdmans, 1998), 161, discussing Luther.

Indeed, in all our acts of prayer, praise and service together, we direct our lives to the Father as Jesus did, in a return to the Father that reflects the Father's own acts of giving to us. Jesus becomes in this way our access to the Father in addition to being the medium and mediator of the Father's gifts to us.[79] Through the Spirit we gain Christ and in and through Christ, with whom we are united, we go to the Father. With Christ, for example, we are able to pray to the Father, the very prayer that Jesus prays to his Father as the Son of the Father in human form. Indeed, in such ways – carried with Christ to the Father – 'God the Father . . . embrace[s] us in his beloved only-begotten Son to become a Father to us.'[80] The Holy Spirit bears our acts of love and praise for the Father to him just as the Holy Spirit in the dynamic life of the Trinity bears the love of the Son for the Father, which is the Father's own love for the Son, back to the Father. Christian experience hereby takes on its own trinitarian form: in the Spirit, who is given to us by the Son, we gain the Son, and through the Son, by the same power of the Spirit, we have a relationship with the Father.[81] In this way, the trinitarian relations in the form of fellowship that were evident in Jesus' own life become ours as well; covenant partnership is elevated to a higher plane in our lives as it was in Jesus' own. The doctrine of the Trinity becomes 'the formal statement of the divine setting of human life:' Since we 'have been adopted to share in Jesus Christ's relationship to the Father in Heaven and to the Father's world,' 'the formula of the Christian life is seeking, finding, and doing the Father's will in the Father's world with the companionship of the Son by the guidance and strength of the Spirit.'[82]

Finally, the way Christ assumes our lives is mirrored in our relations with others as we live a life of service to God's ends. Extending the way Christ took on us sinners for our good, we are to take on the needs of others in order to serve them, in order to extend to them the gifts that Christ extends to us. 'Everyone should "put on" his neighbor

---

[79] This is the emphasis of Torrance in 'The Mind of Christ in Worship.' See Calvin on Christ's priestly work, *Institutes of the Christian Religion*, Book 2, chapter 15, section 6, 502.

[80] Ibid., Book 3, chapter 1, section 3, 540.

[81] See Leonard Hodgson, *The Doctrine of the Trinity* (New York: Charles Scribner's Sons, 1944), 50, 178; and Welch, *In This Name*, 229, 236.

[82] Hodgson, *Doctrine of the Trinity*, 50, 178.

and so conduct himself towards him as if he were in the other's place. From Christ the good things have flowed and are flowing to us. He has so "put on" us and acted for us as if he had been what we are. From us they flow on to those who have need of them.'[83]

As Christians we must identify ourselves, immerse ourselves in the world of change, struggle and conflict as the Word did for us, for the sake of the world's own betterment.[84] Just as the incarnation was in history and its effects only evident there, so Christian service is in and of the world and nowhere else. Though we are elevated beyond the world, as Christ was, through the gifts of God, we should use those gifts as Christ did for the world, not holding them simply for ourselves but being the means of their distribution to others.

We do not, however, assume the needs of others in the place of Christ. We do not come to others as Christ, but as people in the very same situation as those we hope to serve: all of us have the same need of the gifts that come through assumption by Christ.[85] Consequently, 'the real beginning of service is when we see ourselves completely linked to the other with no remnant of superiority.'[86] We identify with others and want to help them because we know we are in the same situation as they are, because we are in need of Christ's help in the same way as they are. 'Remember those who are in prison, as though you were in prison with them' (Heb. 13:3, NRSV).[87]

Of ourselves we are just what they are; only in Christ are we any different and that by a power that remains Christ's and not our own. Making their needs our own we do not, then, purport to purify, heal or elevate them by our good works; the works of Jesus' perfect humanity have that power, but our works, short of the eschaton, remain that of graced sinners. Our action in and for the world is incorporated in the triune God's beneficent action for the world in Christ, but God's action must always surpass our own if it is to be the source of our still sinful action's ongoing purification and renewal. In and of themselves,

---

[83] Martin Luther, 'The Freedom of a Christian,' trans. W. Lambert, in *Three Treatises* (Philadelphia: Fortress Press, 1970), 309.

[84] See, for example, Zizioulas, *Being as Communion*, 224–5, 254–5.

[85] See Barth, *Ethics*, 403–40.

[86] Ibid., 425.

[87] All biblical quotations in my text are from the New Revised Standard Version, unless otherwise noted.

then, our works are simply that – at best good works, not saving ones, often indistinguishable from the acts of non-Christians.[88] By entering into the conflicts and struggles of history for the betterment of the world, we simply hope to be bearing these conflicts and struggles to Christ as the primary source or fountain of their salvation.

Because it is Christ and not ourselves who save, we work in humble solidarity with others for the betterment of the world; for all we know the works of others might be as much a conduit of the Father's gifts through Christ by the power of the Spirit as our own. We tend to identify our assumption by Christ with discrete acts of explicit worship, faith and praise; but, like the assumption of humanity in Christ, our assumption by God, our becoming God's – and God's coming to dwell in us as a result, God's becoming ours – have a kind of invisibility as divine acts; they are known primarily in their effects, in the purifying, healing and elevating love that our acts display.

> It was not by any movement of his that I recognized his coming; it was not by any of my senses that I perceived he had penetrated to the depths of my being. Only by the movement of my heart . . . and . . . because my faults were put to flight and my human yearnings brought into subjection. . . . [W]hen the Word has left me, all these spiritual powers become weak and faint and begin to grow cold, as though you had removed the fire from under a boiling pot.[89]

Should the acts of non-Christians show the same sort of purifying, elevating and healing love – and they arguably do (at least as much as, sometimes more than Christian acts do) – it is presumptuous to limit the workings of God's grace in Christ to explicitly Christian acts of service.[90]

As these last paragraphs suggest, by following a similar structure of argument (with the appropriate permutations depending on the circumstances), one can talk about the relation of church to world, of Christianity to culture, of Christian to non-Christian action, of this

---

[88] See Eberhard Jüngel, 'The Sacrifice of Jesus Christ as Sacrament and Example,' in his *Theological Essays II*, ed. John Webster, trans. A. Neufeldt-Fast and J. Webster (Edinburgh: T&T Clark, 1995), 188–9.

[89] Bernard of Clairvaux, *On the Song of Songs*, Sermon 74, sections 6–7.

[90] See Karl Barth, *Church Dogmatics* IV/3.2, trans. G. W. Bromiley and T. F. Torrance (Edinburgh: T&T Clark, 1962), 604: 'Christ lives indeed in Christians, as He lives in non-Christians, as the Mediator, Head, and Representative of all, as the new and true Adam. . . . [T]here is none who exists wholly without Him, who does not belong to Him, to whom . . . He is not present.'

worldly action to redemption – all in Christological and thereby trinitarian terms.[91] The details will have to await another book. In the next chapter, I turn more directly to the character of Christian action, to an ethics of sorts in keeping with the theological structure of things I have laid out here.

[91] For some interesting suggestions along these lines, see Karl Rahner, *The Christian Commitment* (New York: Sheed & Ward, 1963), chapter 2.

3

The Shape of Human Life

The topic of this chapter is the shape that human life should take, given our theological situation, situated as we are in a theological scheme of things that centers on Christ and the Trinity. United by Christ through the workings of the Spirit, our lives, we have said, are to be formed according to the mode of Jesus' own life, the mode of the second Person of the Trinity, and thereby incorporated within the workings *ad extra* of the Trinity. But what form of life is that?[1]

The fundamental question of ethics – the question how to live – is, then, at the heart of a theology concerned, as this one is, with God as the source and securer of good gifts. The whole economy of creation and salvation concerns ethics in that the distribution of goods and the struggle of those goods for existence over and against the evils that obstruct them are at issue.

One might begin this discussion of theological ethics by asking what our lives are for, theologically conceived. Why have we been created?

[1] This chapter will make clear, for example, that 'the mode of the Son' has nothing fundamentally to do with the obviously masculine connotations of the term. That the language of Sonship was not devised with that intent – but only to suggest, for example, a unity of nature with the first Person and the existence of the second from and with the first – see Richard Norris, 'The Ordination of Women and the "Maleness" of Christ,' in *The Feminine in the Church*, ed. Monica Furlong (London: SPCK, 1984), 79. See also, as an original source, Gregory of Nyssa, 'Against Eunomius,' trans. H. Wilson, *Nicene and Post-Nicene Fathers*, vol. 5 (Peabody, Massachusetts: Hendrickson Publishers, 1994), 112, 114–16, 124, 146, 205, 207, 338. As Karl Barth says in *Church Dogmatics* IV/1, trans. G. W. Bromiley and T. F. Torrance (Edinburgh: T&T Clark, 1956), 210: 'Applied to this "Son" [Jesus Christ] it [i.e., the term "son"] is in a certain sense burst wide open, and can be thought through to the end only as we bring into it meanings which it cannot have in any other use which we can make of it.'

For what purpose? What ends are we to serve? My theological anthropology appears, indeed, to be a task- or vocation-oriented one. The Son is sent by the Father in the power of the Spirit to bring us into the gift-giving relations enjoyed among members of the Trinity; living our lives in Christ according to the mode of the Son, should involve, then, our own service to that mission, spreading the gifts of the Father that are ours in Christ, empowered by the Son's own Spirit.

While this is all true, my incarnation-centered Christology, and account of the Trinity as an overflowing superabundant source, undercut in fundamental ways the usual presuppositions of such task-oriented questions.[2] In the final analysis, God does not so much want something *of* us as want to be *with* us.[3] God does not really need us *for* anything. There is nothing yet to achieve beyond what God's own trinitarian perfection already instantiates. In giving rise to the creature and elevating it to God's own level, God is always bringing about something less rather than something more than what the triune God already is in itself.[4] Without hopes of any advance on God's own goodness thereby, God's gifts to the creature are a kind of love-filled non-purposive or gratuitous trinitarian overflow – something like the aura or penumbra that a generously fecund sun gives off for nothing into the surrounding darkness of space. 'The Divine Existence. . . . extends Its goodness by the very fact of Its existence into all things . . . as our sun, through no choice or deliberation, but by the very fact of its existence, gives light to all those things which have any inherent power of sharing its illumination.'[5] This giving serves no point beyond the fact of it, one might say: to see God's own giving nature reflected in what is not God – in the creature and the creature's action. God gives simply so that there might be a non-divine reflection of what God is.

---

[2] For more on my own position here, see Kathryn Tanner, 'Why are We Here?' in *Why are We Here?*, ed. Ronald Thiemann and William Placher (Harrisburg, Pennsylvania: Trinity Press International, 1999), 5–16.

[3] See Karl Barth, *Ethics*, trans. G. W. Bromiley (Edinburgh: T&T Clark, 1981), 462.

[4] Remember, from chapter 1, Bonaventure's references to creation as no more than a point in comparison with the vast expanse of God's own goodness. See Bonaventure, *Itinerarium Mentis ad Deum*, chapter 6, section 2; and *Collationes in Hexaemeron*, eleventh collation, section 11.

[5] [Pseudo] Dionysius the Areopagite, 'The Divine Names', trans. C. E. Rolt, in *The Divine Names and The Mystical Theology* (London: SPCK, 1940), 86–7.

God does not even need creatures to be with him in this way. It is not just that God does not need us to do something for 'him;' God does not need us at all. God does not need us for company; the trinitarian Persons have all they need in and among themselves.

> Everything that the creature seems to offer Him – its otherness, its being in antithesis to Himself and therefore His own existence in co-existence – He has also in Himself as God. . . . Without the creature He has all this originally in Himself, and it is His free grace . . . if He allows its existence as another, as a counterpart to Himself, and His own co-existence with it. In superfluity – we have to say this because we are in fact dealing with an overflowing, not with a filling up of the perfection of God which needs no filling.[6]

God's relations with us from creation to consummation are the purely gratuitous acts of beneficent love extended outwards to us.

In a similar fashion, an incarnation-centered Christology emphasizes the fact that God does not so much require something of us as want to give something *to* us. Our lives are for nothing in the sense that we are here simply to be the recipients of God's good gifts. Thus, the gift of our assumption into the life of Christ through the power of the Holy Spirit is the presupposition and continual foundation of all our action in the mode of the Son, just as the incarnation was the supporting condition of the sort of life Jesus led. We do not have to achieve anything as a requirement for inclusion in Christ's own life. The acts of ours that initiate and maintain relationship with Christ are brought about by the workings of the Holy Spirit and are acts that point away from our own powers and capacities to Christ and what he has already done for us. Nor are our achievements, particularly in the realm of morals, a requirement for sustaining our assumption by Christ. However good or bad our lives, whether our lives reflect our assumption by Christ adequately or not – most certainly, mostly not – by the power of the Spirit we continue to lead them in Christ.

Within this non-purposive context, however, purposive action, our action for ends, maintains its proper place. The already replete triune God may not need anything from us, but the world does, especially in so far as it is our very sinful actions that hinder the world's reception of God's gifts. We are called to act in a process primarily of self-

6 Barth, *Church Dogmatics* IV/1, 201.

reformation in service of God's ends for the whole world that the superabundant God wants to be similarly replete with goods.

If God shares God's triune life with us, that is a dynamic life, a life of action. Incorporated within the indivisible workings of the Trinity *ad extra* through Christ our lives are similarly set in motion. The relation between Son and Father as that is expressed in Jesus' own life is

> a dynamic and not a static relation; it consists in an activity originating with the Father and manifested in the Son. It may be described as obedience . . . or imitation . . . but at bottom it is nothing so external . . . It is the sharing of one life.
>
> As the love of the Father for the Son, returned by Him in [activity], establishes a community of life between Father and Son, which exhibits itself in that He speaks the Father's word and does his works, so the disciples are loved by Christ and return His love in [action]; in so doing, they share His life, which manifests itself in doing His works.[7]

We, in short, engage in an active fellowship or partnership with the Father through our union with Christ the Son and in Christ's Spirit.

Reflecting in our lives the goodness of God's own triune being, we do so as the free active agents we are. Our agency is part of the gifts God gives in imitation of God's own dynamic life; we reflect, then, the goodness of God in those actions. All creatures reflect the goodness of God simply in being what God gives them to be; humans, at their best, reflect the goodness of God by a self-conscious, and freely chosen active alignment of what they are with God's gift-giving to them. In that specific way, they are the image of God. Thus,

> it will not be difficult to decide the purpose of the whole law: the fulfillment of righteousness to form human life to the archetype of divine purity. For God has so depicted his character in the law that if any man carries out in deeds whatever is enjoined there, he will express the image of God, as it were, in his own life. For this reason, Moses, wishing to remind the Israelites of the gist of the law, said: 'And now, Israel, what does the Lord your God require of you, but to fear the Lord . . . , to walk in his ways, to love him, to serve him with all your heart and with all your soul, and to keep his commandments?' [Deut. 10:12–13] . . . Here is the object . . . : to join man by holiness of life to his God, and, as Moses elsewhere says, to make him cleave to God [cf. Deut. 11:22 or 30:20].[8]

---

[7] C. H. Dodd, *The Interpretation of the Fourth Gospel* (Cambridge: Cambridge University Press, 1953), 194, 195–6.

[8] John Calvin, *Institutes of the Christian Religion*, ed. J. O'Neill, trans. F. Battles, vol. 1 (Philadelphia: Westminster Press, 1960), Book 2, chapter 8, section 51, 415.

Our assumption by Christ has as its whole point such a correspondence in action between Christ's life and ours: we are to live our lives in community with Christ's life as that is demonstrated in all that we think, feel and do.[9] Our lives are to be the reflection in action of our assumption into Christ, in virtue of their taking on the mode of Sonship. Our assumption in Christ is to become visible as our lives show forth, in action and in deeds, the form of Christ's own life, the mode of Sonship. Thereby, the glory of God's own triune superabundance shines forth, not in a static epiphany, but from all that it is that we do for the good, from our efforts to instantiate and further the good of others.

> Glorifying and honouring God can only mean 'following' (or imitating) Him. . . . To give honour to God means that in our existence, words, and actions we are made conformable to God's existence; that we accept our life as determined by God's co-existence. [We are] no longer to live our own lives to ourselves, but to live them to the end that the being of God in all its perfections can find in them a sign and likeness. . . . [T]he way and theatre of the glorification of God is neither more nor less than the total existence of the creature who knows God and offers Him his life-obedience.[10]

Our lives, moreover, do not immediately reflect our assumption by Christ. Indeed, assumed by Christ as active sinners, our lives reflect it far less than Christ's own life did from the start. Our assumption by Christ initiates a struggle to be what our humanity has already become in Jesus. Assumption by Christ sets us the hard task of leading lives actively reformed, purified, and elevated beyond their otherwise sinful ways.

Finally, we are purposive agents within this non-purposive context of God's superabundant gift-giving, because our passivity before Christ does not translate into passivity on any ordinary construal of

[9] See Karl Barth, *Church Dogmatics* IV/3.2, trans. G. W. Bromiley and T. F. Torrance (Edinburgh: T&T Clark, 1961), 594, 597–99; and his *The Christian Life*, trans. G. W. Bromiley (Grand Rapids, Michigan: William B. Eerdmans, 1981), 90, for this understanding of a common life with Christ.

[10] Karl Barth, *Church Dogmatics* II/1, trans. G. W. Bromiley and T. F. Torrance (Edinburgh: T&T Clark, 1957), 674–5. See also G. Berkhouwer, *Faith and Sanctification* (Grand Rapids, Michigan: William B. Eerdmans, 1952), 110, 157–60, 179, who uses glorification and transfiguration language to discuss sanctification with a Western theological emphasis on holy action.

that.[11] Passivity before Christ hardly means our lives are taken out of our hands; it hardly forms an easy contrast with a modern emphasis on human responsibility for the character of our lives. We are assumed by Christ, but what is assumed is the selves that we are in our deeds. We receive from Christ in and through the power of his Spirit but we so receive as the free agents we are. Christ forms us but what is so formed is our action.

The priority that Christ's assumption of us has over the reflection of that fact in our lives suggests no lessening of our lives' active character. Assumption by Christ cannot be identified with discrete moments of our lives in which we are merely passive; it does not divide our lives into a metaphysically or empirically passive component (say, the passive constitution of our very persons or characters); and an active one (say, the expression of such a character in our deeds). One should not maintain, for example, that in being justified God alone acts and that we begin to act only in the process of sanctification.[12] Instead, both divine and human activity are present on both sides. God acts as much when we are united with Christ as when we act in conformity with that fact. In Christ, we find God's action as a presupposition for both aspects of our lives: we are assumed by Christ because Jesus' humanity has already been assumed by the Word; we are sanctified because Jesus' humanity has already been sanctified through the assumption of his humanity by the Word.[13] And our activity falls on both sides, though always doing what it is doing only through the power of God.

Assumption by Christ in the Spirit therefore should not be identified with moments in our lives when our agency is replaced or interrupted by God's. As was the case with the assumption of Jesus' humanity by the Son of God, to say that is to bind God's workings to the usual contrasts between activity and passivity in our lives, in violation of God's transcendence. Instead, the whole of our lives as agents of our

---

[11] See the comparison of Luther and Barth in Eberhard Jüngel, 'Gospel and Law,' in his *Karl Barth: A Theological Legacy*, trans. G. Paul (Philadelphia: Westminster Press, 1986); and the comparison of Luther, Barth, and Jüngel in John Webster, *Barth's Moral Theology* (Grand Rapids, Michigan: William B. Eerdmans, 1998), chapters 8–9.

[12] See Berkhouwer, *Faith and Sanctification*, 93.

[13] See Karl Barth, *Church Dogmatics* IV/2, trans. G. W. Bromiley and T. F. Torrance (Edinburgh: T&T Clark, 1958), 514, 517, 519, 520–1.

own persons is shaped from beyond itself. As Karl Barth draws out this implication of divine transcendence: Although the terms are used, in what is being discussed here,

> the familiar antithesis between spontaneity and receptivity . . . does not occur. When the Reformers described faith as 'a strictly passive matter' (*res mere passiva*), they did not mean that faith included only one aspect . . . – receptivity but not spontaneity. There is no receptivity without spontaneity as well, and faith cannot of course be reduced to some sort of trance-like condition. No, reason's normal activity is not interrupted; but it is directed, guided and ordered by something superior to itself, something that has no part in its antithesis. Taken as a whole (as activity spontaneous and receptive) reason is passively related to that superior reality. It is related to it, in other words, obediently.[14]

Unlike the case with Christ himself, our assumption by Christ can be indexed to some extent to certain discrete moments in our lives, since we are assumed by Christ after the fact of our existence, since assumption by Christ falls within lives that are already being led. But any discrete acts of ours in which the Holy Spirit works to unite us with Christ – faith, baptism, prayer, the preaching and hearing of the gospel message – are still our acts; they differ from other acts not in the cessation of human activity but in their extrospective shape, their attention to what is being done by God for us. All our acts, moreover, should take the same shape.

> Christians live spiritually as and to the extent that they live *ec*-centrically. What are they in and of themselves but . . . sinners . . . fallen victim to death? They can only look beyond themselves, clinging to God himself, and to God only in Christ, and this only as they are freed to do so, and continually freed to do so, by the Holy Spirit.[15]

At our most active – say, in loving service to our neighbors – what we are doing should reflect, then, our empowerment to so act by our assumption by Christ in the Spirit. The grace of God can and should be a focal point of our struggle to lead good lives just as it is the whole point of certain acts of ours, say, faith and prayer. Working for the good we should always be mindful of our failings, seek remission for them, pray for the continual renewal of our efforts in the power of

---

[14] Karl Barth, 'Fate and Idea in Theology,' in *The Way of Theology in Karl Barth*, ed. H. M. Rumscheidt (Allison Park, Pennsylvania: Pickwick Publications, 1986), 54.

[15] Barth, *Christian Life*, 94.

Christ's Spirit, and look ahead to a life of perfect correspondence with God's action for us in imitation of Christ's own glorified life which precedes and empowers us for it.[16]

That, assumed by Christ, our activity is *free* becomes evident from the nature of our imitation of Christ's life, the nature of our correspondence to it. We are not called to slavishly imitate the events of Jesus' life; there is no need for that. What Jesus does to save us is done by him for us so that we need not repeat it. For example, sin and death are overcome by the Son's assumption of death and sin on the cross; should we suffer at the hands of those resisting the Father's mission of beneficence we need not suffer this for the sake of the same saving purpose. Moreover, we need not slavishly imitate the events of Christ's life because Christ is ours in any case. We do and suffer with Christ all that Christ did and suffered whether or not something like those events recur in our own lives, whether or not, for example, something like a crucifixion occurs in our lives as a consequence of our joining Christ in his mission for others. We are crucified with Christ in any case because we are united with him as the crucified one, because the whole of his life becomes our own in our being assumed by him.

Rather than expect a repetition of Jesus' life in our own, when we are assumed by Christ, it is our lives as the contemporary people we are who are so assumed and transformed thereby according to the form of Christ. We follow Christ where he leads in our own lives, shaped as those lives already are by the forces of contemporary times and cultures. Christ's life is extended in new directions as it incorporates our lives within it. Though the mode of Sonship will carry across all differences of space and time, exactly where we will be led in Christ is not easily foreseen from the specifics of Jesus' own life as those reflect an historical distance of two thousand years. Assumed by Christ as Jesus' humanity was assumed by the Son of God, we must do as Jesus did and live out a union with God in ways appropriate to our own circumstances.[17]

What we see here on the topic of human freedom – that imitation of Christ is only properly understood when Jesus' life is not abstracted

---

[16] See Berkhouwer, *Faith and Sanctification*, 121–2, 109–12.

[17] See Edward Schillebeeckx, *Christ: The Experience of the Lord* (New York: Crossroad, 1981), 641.

from incarnation and from the saving point of that – helps clarify the import of imitating Christ on a number of other fronts. For example, we should not make Jesus' holiness in abstraction from the incarnation an object for our imitation through the power of the Spirit. As we saw in the first chapter, Jesus' sinlessness is not a static property for our imitation, but something that takes shape in a process of overcoming temptation as that process is empowered by the fact of Jesus' being the Word incarnate. Jesus does not have his perfection as an achieved state, short of his resurrection, and certainly neither will we, assumed by Christ and battling active sin through the Spirit of Christ that thereby indwells us. We have thus achieved perfection only eschato-logically; it is ours now only as we live in Christ's own glorified humanity, and will be our very humanity's own only when its reforma-tion according to the form of Christ is complete – something that never appears to us to be finally the case. If Jesus' humanity is nevertheless perfect from the first – despite his formation in sinlessness in a process over time – this perfection must be nothing like that of a moral hero or moral virtuoso.[18] It seems, on the contrary, to be the perfection of someone wholly devoted to the Father's cause, someone ever recog-nizing his need as a human being, grateful for what he has received and willing in prayer to call upon the Father's help as the source of all good for his own sake and that of others. If Jesus' perfection as an agent cannot be understood apart from the assumption of his humanity by the Son of God or apart from his relation to the Father, then neither should ours. Short of an achieved perfection that is ours only eschatologically, we are sanctified through life in Christ not in virtue of being morally perfect but in virtue of the eccentric, God-word reference of our efforts, clinging to Christ in the Spirit, and invoking the Father's aid in union with Christ, in our dedication to the Father's own mission of beneficent gift-giving.[19]

When Jesus' life is not abstracted from his humanity's assumption by the Word and its soteriological point, the call to imitate Christ, to correspond in action to Christ's own life, also moves away from any simple valorization of self-denial or self-sacrifice. The sacrifices made

---

[18] See Karl Barth, *Church Dogmatics* I/2, trans. G. W. Bromiley and T. F. Torrance (Edinburgh: T&T Clark, 1956), 156–8.
[19] See Barth, *Christian Faith*, 93.

in Christ can no longer be primarily identified with Jesus' passive sufferings on the cross. The sacrifice that the Son of God makes by assuming all aspects of human existence in a state of suffering and sin to be his own and the sacrifice that the human being Jesus makes in remaining in solidarity with us suffering sinners despite his unity with the Son, range over the course of Jesus' life, in all that Jesus does or undergoes.[20] These sacrifices should be matched in the whole of our own lives as re-directed by the beneficent mission of the Father.[21] We are to immerse ourselves in the struggle and trouble of the world for the good's sake. The sacrifices of Christ's life, broadly construed now, are not, furthermore, good in and of themselves. They are such only 'economically,' as the patristic writers would say, only as a means to overcoming the very sin and suffering to which they are a response.[22] There is nothing good about suffering in a narrow sense, then, apart from efforts to carry out the Son's beneficent mission of the Father, which the Son has shared with us. The suffering undergone by those dedicated to the Father's cause is, moreover, the product of the world's opposition to it, the product of sin's refusal of that beneficence; that suffering is not itself, therefore, a good gift from God. And, finally, such suffering is not self-sacrificial in Christ's life and therefore neither should it be in ours. Jesus' own humanity is exalted and perfected by the sacrifices of Jesus' life; he is not merely acting for others, at the expense of himself.

But, now, if Jesus' whole life is marked by a form of lowliness or humiliation for our sakes (as I seem to be suggesting) is that not the very mode of the Son's existence that we are to share? Again, it is important to see that this is the mode of the Son for a saving purpose or economically; no need to read lowliness into the Son's relation to the Father *per se* as Karl Barth does.[23] The mode of the Son is the form of the Father's gift-giving; we are to share in those gifts of the Father as the Son does through the Son who is Jesus Christ. Sharing in them we are raised in the Son to the Father. Humiliation is not,

---

[20] This is the sacrifice of incarnation discussed in chapter 1, and the sacrifice of Jesus' solidarity with the lowly despite his existence as the Son – his use of his privileges to meet the needs of others.

[21] See Berkhouwer, *Faith and Sanctification*, 139.

[22] See Schillebeeckx, *Christ*, 696, 699–70.

[23] See Barth, *Church Dogmatics* IV/1, 203–4; and IV/2, 343–4.

therefore, the Son's or ours in perpetuity; it is a means to elevation. The Son humbles himself, Jesus humbles himself, to be with us in the lowliness of our suffering and need, in order to save us from it, not to engrave that lowliness into the world as its final good.

There is a kind of humility that is to characterize our lives in Christ as it characterized his own – the humility of a constant reference to God's grace for what we are in our lives, a constant reference to the gift-giving Father who makes those gifts ours through the Son's assumption of humanity as his own. We recognize sin as our own and that our salvation comes only in Christ who is what we are not, Son of God and perfect human partner in fellowship with Father and Spirit as one with the Son. We therefore repudiate the sin of wanting to be ourselves, and to be perfect as ourselves, independently of God's giving to us. To the extent that we are anything but sinners we give the glory to God; Christ is the subject of those acts more than we are. Yet, living in Christ as we do, our humility is not primarily that of mere sinners; it is the humility of those exalted through God's free gift; the humility of the prodigal son not in his profligacy but as welcomed home and inheriting the Father's fortune despite himself, humility in the form of startled gratitude.[24]

But glorifying the Father as gift-giver is too formal a characteristic to simply be the mode of the Son's existence in which our lives are to share.[25] Giving the glory to God is a formal, almost meta-level characteristic of Christian lives. One can give the glory to God whatever it is that one is doing; it tells one nothing very specific about the shape of those lives for which one is to give the glory to God.

The impugning of individualism and a modern stress on individual autonomy is an even more egregiously formal conclusion about the character of human life that contemporary theologians commonly draw from our incorporation in the life of Christ and the Trinity.[26]

[24] See Berkhouwer, *Faith and Sanctification*, 128–30.

[25] Here I am disagreeing with John Calvin; see Brian Gerrish's fine discussion of Calvin in this regard, in his *Grace and Gratitude* (Minneapolis: Fortress Press, 1993), 41–8. I am also disagreeing with Barth; see *Church Dogmatics* IV/2, 589–91; and his *Ethics*, 36: 'God . . . can be served only by those who *are* appropriated without being able to boast of *having* appropriated to themselves what is worth boasting about.'

[26] This is one of the emphases in Dumitru Staniloae, *Theology and the Church*, trans. R. Barringer (Crestwood, New York: St Vladimir's Seminary Press, 1980); and John Zizioulas, *Being as Communion* (Crestwood, New York: St Vladimir's Seminary Press, 1993).

Its formality in this case makes it distortive. Jesus only has his existence and character in relation to the Word; we gain our perfection as human beings only in our relation Christ; the members of the Trinity, in whose life together we thereby participate, are only constituted as themselves in virtue of their relations with each other. Doesn't this suggest a general principle for human lives together in their perfection – that the individual is to be him or herself, and for his or her own good, only in relations with others?

If this is anything more than the contemporary platitude that individuals are shaped in whatever excellences they exhibit by the cultures and communities in which they grow, it is dangerous in its abstractness. Made into a counsel against efforts at self-realization or assertion of individual rights against the community, it begs the question about what that community is like. Relations with God are life-affirming and constitutive of one's person for one's own good – and therefore efforts to separate oneself from God are futilely self-destructive – because of God's special character as gift-giver. If human communities are not similarly beneficent and gift-giving to their members, an attack on individual self-assertion is simply not the proper conclusion to draw from the incarnation and Trinity as models for human lives that participate in them.

Indeed, a general counsel against conflict with community, just because of its abstractness, overlooks the conflict that the incarnation and Trinity bring into the world as we begin to transform our lives by way of participation in them. Not just individuals, but the communities of the world – just to the extent they have not been thoroughly reformed by Christ, and that means, for all intents and purposes, all communities always – are what Christ's assumption of us struggles against. The theanthropic existence that is ours in virtue of our assumption by Christ through the power of the Spirit involves conflict between human sin and Christ's Spirit brought together there. Assumed by Christ in the communal existence that constitutes human life, we should, therefore, be engaged in a constant process of purifying and reforming our communal existence. Why might this purification and reformation not proceed, if necessary, by way of a highly conflictual process of individual prophetic rebuke for the sake of a better way of life together? The ideal community shaped by the triune God's assumption of us in Christ – God's kingdom – as far as we can see remains in conflict with the world's communities of death, injustice, poverty and oppression. Jesus was not afraid to sound an individual voice against such communities for the sake of a different way of life and to go to the cross alone in resistance to them.

It is not enough, then, to say that we as individuals are to be constituted by our relations with other people, in imitation of the way that Jesus is constituted as the one he is in unity with the Son, and the way that Father, Son, and Spirit are constituted as the ones they are in virtue of their relations with each other. One must also say what those human relations are to be like. Their shape must also mirror the incarnation and Trinity in virtue of being assumed into them.

Similarly, it is not enough for us to glorify God in all that we say and do, by acknowledging our dependence upon God for the gifts we have received and our lack of attainment apart from God's continual help, making our whole lives a way of thanking and praising God for what has been done for us in Christ. Our action should show its relation to God not simply in the attitude, disposition, or consciousness with which it is done, but in the structure of that action itself. Something about the pattern of that action as well must glorify God. God's glory, the effulgence of God's life and light extended outwards to us, must become visible in action with a similar shape. We glorify God in a pattern of action together that corresponds to God's decision to be with and for us in Christ. We are to be for one another as God the Father is for us through Christ in the power of the Spirit.

Most generally, that pattern of action is one that ministers divine beneficence to others, in correspondence to Jesus' own ministering of the Father's beneficence to humanity – healing, nourishing, attending to the needs of the world – what Jesus did in his own life, a prior ministry that empowers our own.[27]

---

[27] The phrase 'ministers of beneficence' is Gerrish's in *Grace and Gratitude*, 45, following Calvin, for example, in his *Institutes of the Christian Religion*, Book 3, chapter 1, section 2, 538.

Such is the nature of [Christ's] rule, that he shares with us all that he has received from the Father. . . . [H]e equips us with his power, adorns us with his beauty, enriches us with his wealth. These benefits, then, give us the most fruitful occasion . . . to struggle fearlessly against the devil, sin, and death. . . . [J]ust as he himself freely lavishes his gifts upon us, so may, we, in return, bring forth fruit to his glory.[28]

All our action is to be like that of the ministers at the Lord's banquet table, distributing outward, to others, the gifts of the Father that have become ours in and through the Son by the power of the Holy Spirit.[29] Out of the fullness of the Father by way of Christ and in virtue of his Spirit in us, we are to provide others with all good things for their good: 'God promises that those who do His will shall be as a fountain which the water fails not.'[30]

This ministry of divine benefits brings the idea of God's gifts or blessings together with that of discipleship so as to repudiate any self-satisfaction among the happy, so as to avoid all static theodicies of good fortune, as Max Weber would put it – the common danger of theologies that stress God's bestowal of gifts.[31] Discipleship is brought together with blessings in that discipleship, response to the divine call to be the agent of God's own beneficence, is itself in a way the primary blessing, motored as it is by the primary gift of Godself through Christ.[32] And discipleship is brought together with blessings in that the point of this blessing of discipleship is to lead to others: by way of discipleship one helps distribute to the world all the gifts or blessings that follow from that primary gift of Godself – life, beauty, goodness, bounty in the world. Because of this tie with discipleship, blessings take on a dynamic character. The blessed are not those who already have from God everything for their own good, those who give thanks to God for their good fortune, denied to others. Blessings or gifts of

---

[28] Calvin, *Institutes of the Christian Religion*, Book 2, chapter 15, section 4, 499, discussing the blessings of Christ's kingly office for us.

[29] See Gerrish, *Grace and Gratitude*, 151.

[30] Athanasius, 'Four Discourses against the Arians,' trans. J. H. Newman and A. Robertson, *Nicene and Post-Nicene Fathers*, vol. 4 (Grand Rapids, Michigan: William B. Eerdmans, 1957), 317, with reference to Isaiah 58:11.

[31] For discussion of the dangers and ways around them, see Claus Westermann, *Blessings*, trans. K. Crim (Philadelphia: Fortress Press, 1978); and Pedro Trigo, *Creation and History*, trans. R. Barr (Maryknoll, New York: Orbis Books, 1991), chapter 11.

[32] See Trigo, *Creation and History*, 212–13.

God do not yet form an already achieved state or possession for all, the world is no perfect reflection of Christ's own glorified existence; these blessings or gifts, instead, remain to be given to those in need. The poor are blessed, therefore, as those who are to receive blessings.[33] Those rich in Christ are blessed not solely for their own good but for just this distribution of goods to others. That distribution involves, not satisfaction with the status quo, but action against a reality that contradicts what is achieved in Christ's own glorified humanity, it involves resistance to a world of poverty and constriction, greed, and oppression. That world will fight back as it did in Jesus' own time, in an effort to deprive the ministers of divine benefit of every benefit besides that of the divine *dynamis* of their own discipleship. The successful – the blessed in the eyes of the world – are therefore not associated with the blessed of God, as they are in a theodicy of good fortune.

But what does being ministers of God's beneficence mean for relations among human beings? What communal shape does the distribution of these goods take? What pattern of communal interchange does it involve? What shape should life together take if that is its purpose?

Since human community is to reflect the structure of God's own relations with us, the theological scheme of different levels of divine gift-giving that I laid out in the last chapter can be used to construct an answer. Throughout all God's acts of giving, God's gift-giving retains a distinctive shape. That shape can be summarized in terms of a few general principles that are found differently instantiated in the various stages and levels of God's gift-giving. Instantiated in a way appropriate to *human* relations, these principles suggest the structure that human relations are to take as we are incorporated into the triune life of God through Christ, in order to be the ministers of divine benefits.

This rather round-about procedure – abstracting general principles from the repeated structures of God's gift-giving and figuring out their appropriate application to the specifics of a human ministry of benefits – replaces the effort in much contemporary theology to model human

---

[33] Ibid., 215.

relations directly on trinitarian ones.[34] That effort has its definite downsides.[35] Ignoring appropriate differences among levels in the theological cosmos by modeling human relations directly on trinitarian ones, theologians tend either to downplay the difference between social relations and trinitarian ones, or lose a realistic sense of human relationships. On the former tendency, the Trinity is a perfect community of persons in an ordinary sense of persons, in the way you and I are persons. Besides strongly suggesting tritheism, this position makes the analysis of human communities the key to an account of the Trinity; it is therefore not clear what trinitarian relations add to an independently generated set of conclusions about good human community. On the other tendency, human relations are forced into the mold of trinitarian features like co-inherence; in that case, the human qualities, for example, of Jesus' own relations with the Father – a relation of partnership or fellowship between apparent unequals – are overlooked in the effort to show that trinitarian relations like co-inherence are directly demonstrated in his life.

One should avoid modeling human relations directly on trinitarian ones, because trinitarian relations, say, the co-inherence of trinitarian Persons, simply are not appropriate as they stand for human relations. Co-inherence, for example, is just not a possible created good; God does not give this to us as part of a good creation because human beings in their finitude are not able to be interpenetrative as the Persons of the Trinity are. The finitude that prevents interpenetration in human relations is, moreover, not dissolved by God's gifts beyond creation. When humanity is united with the Son in Christ and the Son works together with that humanity in the theanthropic actions of Jesus, when we are united with Christ and act as empowered by his Spirit within us, humanity does not become anything more than finite, its boundaries expanded by making divinity part of its own natural essence. Humanity remains itself in its finitude; it is elevated beyond itself only in its unity

---

[34] Following Nicholas Fedorov, *Le Christ dans la pensée Russe* (Paris: Cerf, 1970), 84: 'The Dogma of the Trinity is our social program.' See, for example, Staniloae, *Theology and the Church*; Zizioulas, *Being as Communion*; Colin Gunton, *The Promise of Trinitarian Theology* (Edinburgh: T&T Clark, 1991); and Leonardo Boff, *Trinity and Society*, trans. P. Burns (Maryknoll, New York: Orbis Books, 1988).
[35] See Claude Welch, *In This Name* (New York: Charles Scribner's Sons, 1952), 253–72.

with what remains other than itself. When the indivisible working of the Persons of the Trinity incorporates us, our relations with the Father in virtue of our union with Christ take on the more external form of fellowship, not co-inherence, in a way that continues to respect the creature's finite boundedness. So incorporated, our lives as ministers of divine benefit have a trinitarian shape: united with Christ we are called to distribute the good gifts of the Father in the power of the Spirit. Rather than look for some more direct parallel to the relations of Father, Son and Spirit, this just *is* the shape that the Trinity takes on the human level. But that is just where we left off in the last chapter; and it does not tell us very much about the shape of relations among human beings when so incorporated in the Trinity through union with Christ.

Some things, indeed, about the shape of human community are implied simply by the idea of our assumption into the Trinity through union with Christ. We are united with one another, we form a community, the church, as we are united in Christ through the power of the Spirit. This is to be a universal community in that the whole world is at least prospectively united with Christ in and through the triune God's saving intentions for the whole world that has always been the object of God's gift-giving, from the beginning. We are brought together in this community without overriding the particularities of our persons; we are united with one another as what we are and remain in our differences. Thus, the Holy Spirit unites us in Christ even as the Holy Spirit encourages the uniqueness of our persons by a diversity of gifts of the Spirit. The Holy Spirit respects our differences while uniting us in Christ in the same way that the Holy Spirit respects and maintains the differences between Father and Son even as it attests to and bears the love of the Son back to the Father.[36] But, again, the structure of human relations is not very clear here; we are united with each other in so far as we are united with Christ in the Spirit, but what are our relations with *each other* like?

If those relations are structured in a way that reflects the character of God's own gift-giving, they should be marked by unconditional

---

[36] See Staniloae, *Theology and the Church*, 94, 103, 106; and his *The Experience of God*, trans. I. Ionita and R. Barringer (Brookline, Massachusetts: Holy Cross Orthodox Press, 1994), 269.

giving – that is, giving that is not obligated by prior performance and that is not conditional upon a return. This is a first principle of sociability or relationality, derived from the theological structure of things as I have described them, which is general enough to cover both God's relations with us, in all their diversity, and our relations with each other. It marks these relations off from all '*do ut des*' giving – 'I give so that you will give,' the alternative principle that covers barter, commodity exchange, and debtor/creditor relations – the common currency of the distribution of goods in our world, which Christians are called and empowered to revise through an ongoing process of purification.

God does not give gifts to us because of what we have done to deserve them. They are not payments for services rendered. These gifts are not owed by the fulfillment of some prior condition. God gives us all that we are as creatures and therefore prior to these gifts of created goods, there is nothing to us to obligate God's giving them. God sets up covenant relations with Israel, in which God gives Godself in partnership, unilaterally, from sheer free beneficence and not because of this particular people's special merits.[37] Gifts of unity with God in Christ, participation in the triune life of God, are given because of our need, our sufferings and incapacities, not because of our righteousness and bountiful living in communities where justice and peace reign, not because of our good use of gifts already given.

Neither are God's gifts to us predicated upon a return being made for them. Such a return is impossible in any case and therefore God does not give in expectation of it. One cannot pay God back for what God has given because God already has all that one might want to give back. The triune God already has, and in greater abundance, with

---

[37] For discussion of the complicated question of the relation between conditional and unconditional aspects of covenant in the Hebrew Bible, see Jon Levenson, *Sinai and Zion* (San Francisco: Harper, 1985); and Walter Brueggemann, *Old Testament Theology* (Minneapolis: Fortress Press, 1992), 1–44. Any theology of covenant based on this material must show the way two sorts of covenant – unilateral and bilateral – are integrated. I am suggesting a unilateral establishment of covenant, which determines a way of life for God's people. As will be developed in chapter 4, the blessings of covenant are conditional on the pursuit of that way of life, but not the covenant itself with God, who remains faithful to it, ever calling Israel back to that way of life which brings blessings.

a fullness unimaginable, all that we would like to present in exchange. In this way, God's giving to us is unconditioned by hopes of a return, in imitation of the gift-giving relations among Father, Son, and Spirit: the Father does not give to the Son in hopes of a return since the Father already has everything that the Son could possibly return.

One also cannot pay God back for what one has been given because there is nothing more for us to return than what God has already given us. The whole of us – as created and saved – is God's gift in imitation of the way the whole of Son and Spirit are given by the Father. There is nothing more to us, we have nothing more that is simply our own, to give back as payment; we can only give back gifts received. All our gifts to God take on the character then of Eucharist offerings; we offer up to God the bread and wine that are already God's gifts to us as creator, empowered to do so by the gifts already received by humanity in Christ.

God does give to us with the expectation that this giving will be reflected in all that the creature is and does. In the case of humans, this reflection is to be a matter of intentional agency, of our conscious response to God's giving in appropriate words and deeds. Given the invisibility of God's action as creator and savior, this sort of reflection is not, however, forced; God's gifts are not put forward in a way that demands conscious response. God's gifts efface themselves in their giving because God's gift-giving, unlike any gift-giving among creatures with which we are familiar, is total, productive without remainder of its recipients. Because we *are* these gifts, we are not aware of having received them, as we would be in any ordinary case of gifts transferred from someone else's hands to us. Recognition of these gifts is itself, then, a gift from God.

Oriented around God's gift-giving relationship with us, our affections, cognitive faculties, volitions and deeds should all become a register of that relationship. But this way of life is not an obligation, or the fulfillment of a debt, to God. It is simply the only way of life appropriate to the way things are; it is simply our effort, as Karl Barth would say, to be what we already are.[38] Rather than anything God contracts from us through gifts to us, it is our free and joyful testimony

---

[38] Barth, *Ethics*, 404, 462.

and acknowledgment, our act of thankfulness and praise for what God already is in relation to us.

God does give to us in hopes that our lives will reflect God's giving, but God's giving is not conditional on that sort of return being made by us. We do not forfeit God's gift-giving relations with us by not reflecting back to God what God gives, in even this most qualified form of payback. God maintains a gift-giving relation with us however fragile the exhibition of those gifts in our lives or corrupt our performance in response to their being given. As God's creatures, a continuing relationship with God is the condition of our continuing to live, move and breath; if we continue to have the time and space of this created existence, despite our failings and desperate lives in which the reception of God's gifts is blocked, God must be maintaining this gift-giving relationship with us from God's side. Despite the fact that our lives do not reflect God's gift-giving, God still gives and is willing to give more. God indeed establishes a covenant with Israel – a gift greater than mere creation, more than anything that createdness requires – and maintains a steadfast faithfulness to it, again from God's side, whether or not God's human partners manage to live in ways appropriate to it. Again, God gives unity with Godself in Christ even to sinners, indeed especially to them; they 'deserve' these gifts simply because they need them. The gift of union with Christ remains ours, moreover, however short we come in the effort to reflect what it should mean for the lives we lead.

God's gifts can be blocked by our sins and the sins of others against us; but God does not stop giving to us because we have misused and squandered the gifts that God has given us. God's gifts are not on loan to us on the condition that we use them rightly, failures in attentive stewardship thereby bringing their forfeiture. Our sins interrupt the reception and distribution of God's gifts, bringing suffering and death in their train; but these effects are not God's punishment of us, an interruption of God's good favor, in response to our failings. They are merely the natural consequences of turning away from God's bounty which continues to stream forth to us in the way it always has.[39]

[39] See, for this re-reading of suffering and death as punishments, Paul Ricoeur, 'The Interpretation of the Myth of Punishment,' in his *Conflict of Interpretations* (Evanston, Illinois: Northwestern University Press, 1974), 368–77: 'if sin . . . is the expression of . . . separation,

Properly reflecting relationship with God means, then, overcoming sin, becoming plastic once again (as Irenaeus would say) to God's giving of the good. Becoming this proper reflection requires more unmerited gifts in and through Christ; God supplies from out of God's stores even the missing condition of blessings (holiness of life) which is to be our own contribution to the relationship. Rather than offer something in return, we are to remain open in gratitude for the reception of further gifts of God, inexhaustible in their fullness. God obliges, offering gifts for gifts, gifts for squandered gifts, 'rewarding' us anyway despite our inability to make a return, our inability to offer anything besides a willingness to receive more, 'rewarding' us with new gifts that remedy even our failure to offer this non-offering of grateful openness to God's further giving.

The fact that God cannot be repaid in principle and never by us sinners does not then establish an infinite, unpayable debt, one, say, that only God could pay on the cross. Jesus is not punished in our stead; God simply does not punish in that way in response to sin.[40] Nor does the cross save by paying back to God in a positive way the obedience that God's gift of the law or a way of life requires, the Son of God in Christ taking our place as God's for once obedient partner.[41] There is no such requirement of obedience as a condition of God's good favor. God saves through unity with the Son in Christ. Jesus' obedience to the Father – a life that reflects the Father's beneficent will for us – is an effect of that unity with the Son, not the very condition of our being saved by Christ. The humanity of Jesus is not blessed by God, in a way that extends the blessings of God to all of us,

---

then the wrath of God can be another symbol of the separation, experienced as threat and active destruction . . . punishment is nothing more that the sin itself . . . it is not what a punitive will makes someone undergo as the price of a rebel will . . . punishment for sin is the sin itself as punishment, namely, the separation itself" – which the Old Testament often discusses in terms of suffering and death (371).

Saying that death is a natural consequence of separation from God as life giver and provider of all good things is not to say that mortality is unnatural. Mortality might be part of human nature; whether (and how) we in fact die (or not), and whether we remain so, are matters dependent on the character of our relation to God. I will say more about this in chapter 4.

[40] I am here disagreeing with the usual interpretation of vicarious punishment, which is often emphasized in Lutheran accounts of the atonement.

[41] I am here disagreeing with the Calvinist position of Karl Barth.

because Jesus is obedient; Jesus is obedient because his humanity has already been blessed. The cross simply does not save us from our debts to God by paying them. If anything, the cross saves us from the consequences of a debt economy in conflict with God's own economy of grace by canceling it. We are ransomed on the cross from the suffering and oppression in which a debt economy has thrown us; taken from the cross we are returned to our original owner God, to God's kingdom of unconditional giving, snatched out of a world of deprivation and injustice from which we suffer because of our poverty, our inability to pay what others demand of us.[42] In Christ, we see the manner of divine action that the Jubilee traditions of the Hebrew Bible aimed to reflect: debts are forgiven rather than paid, debtors freed from the enslavement that accrues through non-payment, land returned to its original owners despite their forfeiture of any claim to it through unpaid debt to the creditors who had seized it.[43]

This unconditionality of God's giving implies the universal distribution of God's gifts. This is a second principle of relationality, derivable from a theological structure of things centered on Christ. Because it has no pre-conditions, God's giving as creator is universal in scope; everything that is benefits. In Christ, God is clearly the God of sinners as well as the righteous, of the Gentiles who lack God's gift of the covenant as well as the Jews who have the benefit of the law, of the suffering as well as the fortunate, indeed the God especially of the former in that they are the ones in greatest need of God's gifts. There is nothing we need to do or to be in particular in order for God to be giving to us. The distinction between good and bad, between Jew and Gentile – all the distinctions that typically determine the boundaries of human love and concern – fall away in that God gives simply to those in need, in order to address every respect in which they are in need, without concern for anything they especially are or have done to deserve it.

God's giving indeed breaks all the usual boundaries of closed communities. In creating the world, God goes outside the community of the divine Trinity to offer gifts to the stranger, to what is not divine. God offers the gift of Godself in partnership with a people by choosing

[42] See Schillebeeckx, *Christ*, 480–1.
[43] See Sharon Ringe, *Jesus, Liberation, and the Biblical Jubilee* (Philadelphia: Fortress Press, 1985).

those who are deprived and enslaved strangers within the community in which they reside. Jesus aligns himself with those without favor or good standing within the community of God's people; and brings all within the very life of the triune God despite all their differences, despite indeed the greatest difference of all that remains nonetheless, between divine and non-divine.

In order to be proper ministers of God's benefits, we would therefore need to recognize the common right of all to the goods of God, simply as creatures; we would have to recognize our obligation to advance the fortunes of that universal community of creatures that is the object of God's favor. God's giving is not owed to creatures but if those gifts are being given unconditionally by God to all in need, creatures are in fact owed the goods of God by those ministering such benefits, without being or having done anything in particular to deserve them. Our good works, in short, are not owed to God but they are to the world.

Those in need have a rightful claim on the ministers of divine beneficence in imitation of the way the Son and Spirit have by rights of nature what the Father nonetheless gives to them. On an equal footing with the Father, the Son and the Spirit already are by nature what they are given by the Father; in this sense they have by rights of nature what they are given; they are given what is their very own. The humanity assumed by the Word in Christ, though in the needy situation of sin, has by rights of nature the gifts bestowed on it in virtue of its being the Word's very own. Though creatures are never owed anything by God – God's gifts are nothing but gracious here – God's decision to give them everything means an oddly analogous coming together of gift and right. In the creature's case, one is given that to which one has a right in that what one lacks is one's due. Because of God's unconditional beneficence, need determines a right here; we are only giving the needy their due when we try to meet their needs.

The community of concern to human beings as the ministers of divine benefit should therefore be as wide as God's gift-giving purview. In this universal community, humans should try to distribute the gifts of God as God does without concern for whether they are especially deserved by their recipients. Without bothering themselves, for example, with distinctions between the deserving or undeserving poor, they should give their full attention, instead, to the various needs of members of this worldwide community. They must offer special protections, moreover, as these become necessary, to those most likely to be left out of the community of concern at any point in time – the outcasts and strangers in their midst.

Again in imitation of God's relations with us, one gives to others with the hope that these gifts will be the basis for their activity as ministers of divine beneficence; one gives to them for their empowerment as givers in turn. Their failure to do so is not, however, cause for the forfeiture of such benefits. Gifts to them were not conditional on such a return; the absence of it is therefore not grounds for their discontinuation. Their becoming ministers of divine beneficence by way of our gifts is not, moreover, to be considered a return under threat, a payment of a debt, or the meeting of an obligation. It is rather to be hoped for as the natural concomitant of the joyful development of such gifts in thanks for gifts received. One expects dedication to the good of others to arise from the grateful sense that one has already been the recipient of benefit.

Such a hope begins to seem reasonable when one sees how the shape of this community dedicated to addressing the needs of all is further specified by a principle of non-competitive relations that God's gift-giving abides by.[44] So specified, unconditional giving in human relations to meet the needs of all takes on the shape of a community of mutual fulfillment.

Within God's intra-trinitarian life and in God's relations with us, God's gift-giving is non-competitive in that (1) the giver's remaining giftful does not come at the expense of gifts to another, (2) giving to others does not come at one's own expense, and (3) being one's own and having for one's own do not begin where relations of active reception from another end – indeed, we are our own and have for our own only as we, and what we have, are a beneficent other's.

Competitive relations are avoided because gift relations here are not in any usual sense exchanges or transfers. The Father need not begrudge the Son or Spirit anything; the triune God need not begrudge

---

[44] The reader will notice the return of one of the principles outlined in chapter 1.

the world anything; the Word need not begrudge Jesus anything; Jesus need not begrudge us anything, since in giving to all these others nothing is being given away. What is given remains the possession of the one giving. Nothing is transferred, as if these gifts involved the moving of material goods from one site to another. For example, creation involves no simple transfer because there is nothing to us prior to God's giving to receive such a transfer, no one exists prior to God's giving to take the gift in hand; we as a whole are the gift, rather than being the gift's already existing recipients.

Moreover, we never take possession of what is given as if God's giving to us became at some point simply the given, the product of a completed transfer, and therefore simply ours. The gift is never separable from the giver: creatures would not remain what they are without a constant relation of dependence upon God, we are covenant partners with God only to the extent God remains present to us, we have gifts in Christ – say, eternal life – not in and of ourselves in the form of some new 'supernatural' properties, but only as we remain one with Christ in faith and love by the gracious workings of the Holy Spirit. Our coming to be and to act independently of God is never the ground, then, of becoming, and making things, our own. We are our own and have for our own only as what we are and have are God's own.

If our lives together imitate God's giving to us, we should not need to hold what we are or have as our exclusive possessions, or claim with respect to them exclusive rights of use, against others. What the Father has the Son and Spirit also have; the very same thing is repeated in different modes. The three work together as one in that the will to work – its particular shape, general capacities, etc. – is the very same among them in virtue of this identity of substance or essence. What the Son has becomes humanity's own and the reverse, this time not by both reproducing the very same thing in different modes but by virtue of their unity as distinctly different things through the Son's assumption of humanity. Because the human has become God's own by way of the Word's assumption of it, the triune God achieves God's ends – the fullest possible communication of goods to the creature – by appropriating human powers for that end; God saves in and through the living of a human life. Because the human is God's own in this way, the divine becomes the human's own in Christ – that is, Jesus acts by the power of God, with divine effects.

Following this same pattern of non-exclusive possession and rights of use in a way appropriate for human relations, what we have for our own good, others should have as well. Wherever possible that would mean rights of use to the very same things should be shared or common. Where that is not possible – and it is often not possible among finite creatures subject to fundamentally competitive limitations of time and space, creatures who are themselves by not being others – it means everyone having as far as possible in their own persons and lives the distinct goods that others also have in a distinct fashion in theirs. (For example, not everyone can live in my house; but others should be able to live in a comparable one of their own and my doing so should not come at their expense.) In every case, ideally, persons sharing their gifts with others as those others benefit in community from the effects of those gifts' employment – that is the fundamental meaning of a community of mutual fulfillment. (For example, my development of my intellectual talents becomes the gift to others of my teaching and writing, gifts which those others react to and develop in turn in ways that become a gift to me – confirming, altering, radically realigning my own intellectual sense of things by way of their own teaching and writing.)

On this non-competitive understanding of things, being ourselves as the persons we are and having all that we have for our own good should not come at the expense of our being our fellows' own in community. Son and Spirit are themselves, and all that they are for the good, just because they are the Son and Spirit of the Father, the Father's own, and the reverse. Apart from the grace of Christ, we are ourselves, and have all that we have for the good, just to the extent we continue to be the triune God's creatures, ever receiving from the Father's hands of Son and Spirit. What the humanity of Jesus has beyond its created capacities is its own only as the Logos makes that humanity its own by assuming it to itself. What we have in Christ for our perfection and elevation becomes our own only as we are borne by Christ, only as Christ becomes the subject of our predicates, the agent of our own acts. United with Christ, we are ourselves only as we incorporate what is God's very own within ourselves; our acts are perfected only as we act along with and under the direction of God, whose powers become a kind of principle of our own, now compound operation, through the gift of Christ's Spirit. Similarly, our lives as individuals should be constituted and enhanced in their perfections as we share our lives with others in community, identifying ourselves thereby as persons in community with others and not simply persons for ourselves. We perfect one another in community as our operations to perfect our own gifts and talents enter into and supplement the operations of others in a combined venture for goods otherwise impossible.

These relations of non-exclusive possession and self-identification make sense, however, only under very particular preconditions. They presuppose, for example, a very unusual sense of possession or property. Here you are someone else's only in virtue of their giving to you. They 'own' you, you are theirs, only as they give to you for your own good, only as they make you the recipients of their loving concern, not in virtue of their powers to restrict you, take from you, or do with you as they will.

Owning by giving is the way the Son is the Father's own, it is the way humanity is the Son's own, it is the way we are the Father's own. We are the Father's own as his children not his slaves, his children only through a gift and not by nature as the Son of God is, his children not in the sense of those of whom one has the right to make demands but children in whom the Father delights and wills to give his fortune, despite their follies and failings, indeed just for the sake of overcoming those follies and failings.[45] We are to be each others' own in community in this same general sense of possession or property.

Relations of non-exclusive possession and identification only make sense, too (as the reader will remember), where giving to others and having oneself are not in competition with one another. The Persons of the Trinity give to one another without suffering loss; each continues to have what it gives to the others. What the triune God gives to us does not lessen the inalienable fullness of God's own life. God gives to us without that giving being conditional upon a return but God's giving, in short, is not self-sacrificial. What Jesus does for us – say, die on a cross – does not come at his own expense, but is part of the process

---

[45] See Gerrish, *Grace and Gratitude*, 100–1, on Calvin.

of perfecting his own humanity to glory; our humanity is only perfected to the extent his is before us.

We too, then, should give to others out of our own fullness. It is not as the poor that we are to give to others but as those rich, to whatever extent we are, giving to those poor in what we have, in solidarity with them. Jesus entered into our poverty for the sake of the poor but he did so as someone rich with the Father's own love. We do not give of our poverty but of what we have already received so as to work for the good of others in response to their need. Having received gifts ourselves from God and from all those others in whom we are in community through Christ, we give to others, rather than withhold from them, rather than hold what we have simply as our own.

Rather than being in competition with our having something ourselves, having received gifts is in this way the very condition of our giving to others. Self-assertion, the effort to realize one's own perfection and good, therefore need not be at odds with concern for the needs of others. That sort of self-concern is not at odds with it, just to the extent one's own perfections are what enable gift-giving to others.

Following the same theological principle of non-competition, giving to others, moreover, should not mean impoverishing ourselves. Giving away should not be at odds with one's continuing to have. In a community where others are not holding their gifts simply for themselves, presumably what one gave away would come back to one from others.[46] But this is not quite what the theological structure of things suggests; it simply seems that what one gives does not come at one's own expense; one is not giving by a giving away that leaves oneself bereft; what one gives remains in one's possession. A human community conforming to this idea would be a community of mutual fulfillment in which each effort to perfect oneself enriches others' efforts at self-perfection. One perfects oneself by making one's own the efforts of others to perfect themselves, their efforts too being furthered in the same way by one's own. Something like that is happening all the time

---

[46] See Frank Kirkpatrick, *Together Bound: God, History and the Religious Community* (New York and Oxford: Oxford University Press, 1994), chapter 10.

in community living, but it is rarely made a major principle of community reform and self-purification.

Indeed, I do not think either principle of unconditional giving or non-competition is unrealistic as a principle for implementation in human communities – at least as a principle for re-shaping communities already on the ground. Human communities do not have to be divine ones – one need not pretend we are trinitarian Persons in community – to see their point for the lives we already lead. This is not to say, however, that such implementation would be easy: the divine working for our benefit that we try to minister to ever meets resistance in our day as it did in Jesus' time. What we might make of the failure of such a task, in Jesus' day as in ours, brings us to the topic of the next chapter: what is the meaning of efforts that come to nothing?

4

The End

This chapter explores what my systematic theology suggests about the character of Christian hope. Most generally, what are we to expect of our lives in the world? What will come of them? More specifically, how do we make sense of the apparent failure and futility of our efforts to manifest in our lives and carry into the world the gifts of God flowing to us in Christ?

Indeed our lives in Christ seem to come to nothing. Ever struggling against our own sinful impulses, we never exhibit Christ's own perfect humanity. Confirmed in this wariness of Christian failing by a contemporary hermeneutics of suspicion, we have been trained, indeed, to expect fault just where the claim of moral privilege is heard the loudest. Our efforts to minister God's benefits to the world meet, moreover, the constant resistance that Jesus himself met on the cross. Expecting resistance, even defeat, at the hands of the powers of oppression and injustice on the basis of Christ's example and our own past experience, any hopes of world transformation are dashed by the spirit of contemporary cultural pessimism, by a renewed sense, in contemporary times, of structural intransigences. We need no Gregory of Nyssa to convince us that apparent progress forward in world history is really, underneath it all, nothing more than the futile washing in and washing out of waves on a beach.[1] Finally, our efforts

[1] See Jean Daniélou's introduction to *From Glory to Glory: Texts from Gregory of Nyssa's Mystical Writings*, trans. H. Musurillo (Crestwood, New York: St Vladimir's Seminary Press, 1995), 47–53.

at self-reform, no matter how successful, seem wiped away with our deaths, deaths which, as modern people, we suspect are less the wages of sin, in and of themselves, than they are the consequences of our natural existence as creatures. Similarly, the socio-cosmic consequences of our ministering divine benefits to others (which is the forward focus of my systematic theology in particular) will, no matter how far they go, finally come to nothing with the end of human communities and cosmic death. The best scientific description of the day leaves little doubt that death is the end towards which our solar system and the universe as a whole move. Our sun will one day exhaust its fuel, annihilating life on this planet. The universe will either collapse onto itself in a fiery conflagration or dissipate away its energy over the course of an infinite expansion. If the scientists are right, the world for which Christians hold out hope, the world they hope to minister to as the agents of divine beneficence, ultimately has no future. Hope for an everlasting and consummate fulfillment of this world, a fulfillment of the world that would imitate the fullness of the triune life through incorporation into it, seems futile since destruction is our world's end. Because of its cosmic scope, this last failure of hope would bring with it all the others.

One strategy of response to it, often found in the this-worldly, future–oriented eschatologies of today, is for theologians to contest the finality of the world's end, and therefore the completeness of the scientific description of it. This would conform with the way that, when challenged by scientific or other naturalistic understandings of personal death, theologians contest the idea of mortality as a natural fact and therefore its inevitability as the end of finite creatures. If one takes this strategy of response, one could admit that science accurately depicts the fate of the world left to its own devices; what science leaves out of account is the influence of God's working to divert, or overcome, what one could legitimately expect to occur simply from the world's own principles of operation. Thus, a theologian might maintain that the world will not come to the dire pass scientists envision because of the ongoing influence of a good, life-affirming God in world processes generally. Or, a theologian could claim that the world will be led beyond the destruction to which it does indeed come of its own accord by a God who, as

Christians affirm of their creator and redeemer, can bring something from nothing, and life from death. God might indeed use the old world's destruction, as the scientists describe it, as a purgative means to a new heaven and earth beyond the reach of the old world's own capacities; the destruction of the world becomes in that case a kind of world purification by crucifixion signaling the death of death by way of divine power.

Taking this sort of strategy of response leaves the basic shape of a this-worldly, future-oriented eschatology – so common in contemporary theology – unaltered. At most, scientific prediction of a dire future would encourage contemporary eschatologies of this sort to move away from optimistic assessments of what one can expect from natural processes apart from God's help. The consummation of the world is not brought about by the world. A gap exists between the results of world processes and the world's consummation, a gap to be bridged by a God with the power to reverse those results, the power to bring what is otherwise absolutely unexpected into existence – say, a world that knows neither loss nor suffering.[2] Or, a grace-motored continuity, rather than a continuity of purely natural processes, spans the world as we know it and the world to come: the world moves without any great interruption to its consummation but it does so only in virtue of divine powers not its own.[3]

Besides this eschewal or qualification of evolutionary accounts of the world's end, incorporating scientific description within a future-oriented, this-worldly eschatology simply redirects theological interest to certain aspects of the usual story of the world's end. Theologians are inclined to try to describe, with the help of scientific categories, the nature of the transition to the world to come, and the new character of that world. Does, for example, that transition, or the world to come, involve spatial and temporal processes comparable to the ones scientists describe? Is that transition, or the world to come, constituted and formed at least in part by the interactive agencies of finite creatures

[2] See, for example, the position of Jürgen Moltmann in his *The Coming of God*, trans. M. Kohl (Minneapolis: Fortress Press, 1996).

[3] For this viewpoint, see Karl Rahner, 'Immanent and Transcendent Consummation of the World,' trans. D. Bourke, *Theological Investigations*, vol. 10 (London: Darton, Longman & Todd, 1973), 273–89.

in something like the way the present world is?[4] In the world to come, what features of the world might account for its being an everlasting world of perfect fulfillment, a world without death, suffering, loss, or the tragic competition for goods that sets one creature against another?[5]

Another possible strategy for responding to the apparent conflict between scientific end-time scenarios and theological hopes for the future of this world asks what a Christian eschatology might be like if scientists are right that the world does not have a future. Is it really the case that such an end is simply incompatible as it stands with Christian hopes for this world? Might there not be a Christian hope to cope with and make sense of the end of things that scientists describe? A Christian hope that copes with the world's final failure rather than denying it or replacing it with a world no longer marked by failure?

This sort of response to scientific descriptions of the end-time would do for eschatology something comparable to what many theologians have already done for the doctrine of creation in response to scientific (or philosophical) accounts of the world that conflict with Christian descriptions of a beginning of things. In response to that conflict – say, in response to philosophical or scientific arguments for the universe's eternality – theologians did not always feel the need to attack head-on the adequacy of these arguments; they often just gave a broader account of the meaning of creation, one that could be dis-associated from a simple insistence on a beginning to things.[6] On such a new account of creation, the world is the creation of God whether it has a beginning or not and whatever the process of its origination. In the case of a conflict between eschatology and scientific description, one would think that one could, similarly, reinterpret the common

---

[4] See Miroslav Volf, 'Enter into Joy! Sin, Death and the Life of the World to Come,' in *The End of the World and the Ends of God*, ed. John Polkinghorne and Michael Welker (Harrisburg, Pennsylvania: Trinity Press International, 2000), 256–78.

[5] See Moltmann, *Coming of God*, part 4.

[6] Thomas Aquinas is an early figure who suggests the shape of this strategy of response. Although he does dispute the deductive status of philosophical arguments for the eternality of the world in order to make room for the scriptural claim that the world has a beginning (philosophers, according to Aquinas, cannot prove the eternality of the world but make, at best, only a relatively good, probable case for it), Aquinas offers a general account of creation in which nothing much rides on the fact that the world does have a beginning. See his *Summa contra Gentiles*, trans. J. Anderson (Notre Dame, Indiana: University of Notre Dame Press, 1975), Book 2, chapters 18 and 38.

contemporary outlook on eschatology so that it holds whatever the final state of the world, as scientifically described.[7] The fundamental meaning of Christian hopes for the world would have no more stake in whether or how the world ends than a Christian account of creation has in whether or how the world had a beginning (say, by means of a big bang).

One might suspect that such a reinterpretation of Christian claims would mean Christianity's relinquishing of its hold on cosmic questions. Such questions would be turned over to the scientist (or philosopher), leaving Christianity without a say on matters that concern this world. Again, however, the comparable case of creation does not bear this worry out.

Belief in creation can, it is true, be spiritualized as a way of avoiding conflict with scientific descriptions of a beginning of things – say, by reducing the import of creation to a psychological, purely human and private matter. For example, creation might mean nothing more than what it means for Rudolf Bultmann: a sense of the uncanny, of the irretrievable importance of the moment, and of being disposed by a force beyond one's control.[8] When reinterpreted to avoid conflict with scientific and philosophical descriptions of the beginning of things, creation can, however, continue to concern this world and its relation to God, as the classic example of Thomas Aquinas' effort to reinterpret creation in the face of the best Aristotelian science of his day makes clear.[9]

In a move that is typical for most modern theological struggles with scientific description of the world's beginnings, creation for Thomas is de-temporalized, one might say, so that it becomes a relation of dependence on God that everything that exists enjoys in every respect that it is. Such a relation of dependence holds whether the world has a beginning or not. This irrelevance of the question of beginnings suggests nothing other-worldly, subjective or a-cosmic about the account of creation being offered. To the contrary, it is the very

[7] While admitting for both scientific and religious (for example, scriptural) reasons, that the world does end.

[8] See Rudolf Bultmann, 'The Meaning of Christian Faith in Creation,' in his *Existence and Faith*, trans. and ed. Schubert Ogden (London: Hodder & Stoughton, 1961), 206–25.

[9] See Thomas Aquinas, *Summa contra Gentiles*, Book 2, chapter 18.

irrelevance of that question of beginnings that guarantees the cosmic comprehensiveness of the account. If being created means to depend on God, the world that is created is not just the world of the beginning but the world as a whole, across the whole of its duration however long or short that may be, whether with or without a beginning or end.

If one were to reinterpret eschatology in a similar fashion so that considerations of the world's end – the eventual failure of the world's existence and with it all achievement of the good within it – are no longer of paramount concern, presumably the consequences might also be similar to what one finds in the Thomistic case. The consequences would be, in other words, not an other-worldly or spiritualized eschatology that leaves concern for this world behind (say, by the reduction of the content of the claim to human attitudes towards the world), but a more comprehensively cosmic eschatology. Such an eschatology would be comprehensively cosmic in the sense that its preoccupations would not center on the world of the future but on the world as a whole and on an ongoing redemptive (rather than simply creative) relation to God that holds for the world of the past, present and future. What might drop out in response to a conflict with science is not the this-worldly, cosmic character of Christian eschatology but simply its predominantly future orientation.

However, can Christian hopes do without preoccupations concerning the world's future? With the loss of those concerns for the future has not too much been lost? If Christian eschatology does not offer specifically future hopes, what might motivate action to bring in a better future for humans and the planet? Without expectations of a world to come, what disturbs complacency concerning the world as it seems to work now? Without hopes for the future of this world, what can Christian eschatology do to alleviate despair in the face of present injustice and suffering? What is to prevent the sense that all our efforts to better the world are simply futile?

To put the same set of worries another way, has perhaps too much of a modern scientific viewpoint been conceded by the strategy of response I am exploring? What is to prevent such an eschatology from being co-opted by the exterministic cultural concomitants of a belief in cosmic death? Christian eschatology in that case would simply confirm the untoward contemporary understandings of world, self, and community that scientific predictions of the world's end already play into and foment: (1) a nihilistic sense of the futility of efforts to improve the human situation and conditions of the planet – what is the difference if everything is to end in some cosmic crunch? – and (2) an irresponsible, simply self-interested focus on goods that can be had in the moment without much expenditure of effort. As the Bible gives shocked expression to such a view of the moral space of human life:

> They said to themselves in their deluded way: 'Our life is short and full of trouble, and when man comes to the end there is no remedy; no man has ever been known to return from the grave. . . . [C]ome then, let us enjoy the good things while we can, and make full use of the creation, with all the eagerness of youth. . . . Down with the poor and honest man! Let us tread him under foot. . . . For us let might be right!' (Wisdom of Solomon 2:1, 6, 10, NEB).

My explorations, then, of an eschatology for a world without a future will have to have two parts. First, of course, I need to lay out the basic shape of such an eschatology, developed in light of the incarnation-centered Christology of previous chapters. But I also need, in a second step, to explain the main options such a position affords for obligating and inspiring action to further the flourishing of human beings and the planet. How are hopelessness in the face of present trouble, complacent inactivity regarding suffering and injustice, and irresponsible self-concern, to be avoided? In short, absent a vision of this world to come, absent expectation of final success, what motivates and helps sustain action in history for a better world over the long haul? This second part of the project is to make clear, then, how my reinterpretation of contemporary eschatology does not bring with it the loss of eschatology as political theology, the loss of active, socially committed challenge to structures of oppression, injustice, and ecological devastation that is so much a part – and rightly so – of many contemporary eschatologies.

Eschatology for a World that Ends

As parallel modifications in Christian accounts of creation suggest, what is required here is an account of a saving relationship with God that undercuts the religious importance of the question whether the world will end. Just as creation in its essential meaning does not refer to what happens in the beginning (in contradistinction to what happens after), so the central claim of eschatology must not refer to what happens at the end (in contradistinction to what happens before). Understood in that way the eschaton – consummation in the good – would have to do primarily with a new level of relationship with God, the final one surpassing what we are simply as creatures, beyond which there is no other – the relation with God discussed in previous chapters as life in the triune God, as that becomes possible for us through the Father's sending of the Son in Christ by the power of the Spirit. What is of fundamental religious interest for the question of salvation is the character of this relation to God and not what the world is like or what happens to it considered independently of that relation – say, at its end. One retains a religious interest in the future of the world *as it exists in this new relationship with God*, that is, one wants to know what consequences this relationship with God has for the world. But the world has this future whether the world, considered in itself, ends or not and whatever the process by which it does; the world will have this future, irrespective of such events, because it has this future in virtue of the character of its relationship with God. Worries about the end of the world are relativized, that is, undercut by a new theological context of discussion, since the world can enjoy this new level of relationship with God whatever its state, whether or not the world ends, and whatever the process by which it does. The relationship holds whether the world continues to exist or ceases to exist.

To see the sense of these last remarks, it is important to see how life in God is a way of developing some typical biblical moves that already relativize or undercut the religious significance of the difference between biological life and death (or life as existence and death as cessation of existence).[10]

First, there is the dominance particularly in the Old Testament of a wider (so-called metaphorical) use of 'life' and 'death,' where life refers

[10] For the following discussion, see Lloyd Bailey, *Biblical Perspectives on Death* (Philadelphia: Fortress Press, 1979); Rudolf Bultmann, *Life and Death: Bible Keywords from Gerhard Kittel's Theologisches Wörterbuch zum Neuen Testament* (London: A&C Black, 1965); and Eberhard Jüngel, *Death – The Riddle and the Mystery*, trans. I. and U. Nicol (Philadelphia: Westminster Press, 1974), chapter 4.

to fruitfulness and abundance, longevity, communal flourishing and individual wellbeing, and death is a catch-all for such things as suffering, poverty, barrenness, oppression, social divisiveness and isolation. According to these more extended senses of life and death, one can be dead while alive; death enters into the course of life as the threat of such things as sickness, impoverishment, and lack of fulfillment. One can also enjoy a death that imitates life – in old age, surrounded by one's posterity. 'Your descendants will be many and your offspring like the grass of the earth. You shall come to your grave in ripe old age' (Job 5:25–6).

A second, similar sort of relativization of the difference between biological death and life is suggested by Old Testament passages in which 'life' and 'death' seem to refer to the *way* one lives or dies, in particular whether one lives (or dies) for God (and for others). One lives, in this sense, to the extent one dedicates one's life to the God who is the source of life in all its extended senses, to the extent that one keeps faith with a relationship with God by maintaining the form of life that relationship with God requires. All the goods of life – in our first, extended sense of the term 'life' – are blessings that stem ultimately from relationship with God. To die is to break with this life-giving, blessing-bestowing relationship with God and the covenant it forms; to live is just to place oneself willingly and joyfully within it. 'I have set before you life and death, blessings and curses. Choose life that you . . . may live, loving the Lord your God, obeying him, and holding fast to him; for that means life to you and length of days . . .' (Deut. 30:19–20). One can and should hold fast to God whatever the dangers and vicissitudes of life; in this sense one enjoys a gift that cannot be lost, a blessing of life that survives every trial and tribulation, every threat, that is, from the forces of death. Whatever the adversity, one can take comfort in the fact that 'Yahweh is my chosen portion and my cup' (for example, Ps. 16:5), 'my refuge' (Ps. 73:28); indeed, in such circumstances it becomes clear the way God's 'steadfast love is better than life' (Ps. 63:3).

But can the relations with God and neighbor that spell life be sustained across the fact of biological death? (Spiritualizing those relations, in the way the last biblical quotation suggests, can only go so far; it is therefore an ultimately unsuccessful way of relativizing the difference between life and death.) Does death not disrupt one's relationship to the life-giving powers of God? 'I shall lie in the earth; you will seek me, but I shall not be' (Job 7:21). 'For Sheol cannot thank you, death cannot praise you; those who go down to the Pit cannot hope for your faithfulness' (Isa. 38:18). To what extent then does our second sense of life in relational terms genuinely relativize the difference between continued existence and its cessation?

For the Old Testament, the worry I am now raising primarily concerns the effect of biological death on an individual's relation to God. The death of individuals may be final for them but not for the community, which continues to exist in relation to God. Thus, a single generation of the community might be cut off from God and suffer a grievous downturn, but presumably there might still be hopes for the next.

Despite a sense of the finality of death for the individual him/ herself, worries about individual mortality can be quelled in the Old Testament by a more primary concern for the community and by a sense of the dead individual's continuing existence for it – through offspring or communal memory.[11] So, the finality of his own individual death is softened in this way by Jacob on his deathbed: 'I am about to die, but God will be with you, and will bring you again to the land of your ancestors' (Gen. 48:21). One can participate beyond one's death in the ongoing life of the community through one's children, but even 'eunuchs . . . shall receive from me something better than sons and daughters: a memorial and a name in my house' (Isa. 56:3–5, NEB).

This sort of response to the irrevocability of personal death is lost, for us, however; with scientific descriptions of the end-time, all human communities, along with the cosmos itself, seem to suffer as irrevocable a death as any individual person. The problem posed by personal death, in short, is now simply writ large for us. Are there biblical perspectives, particularly Old Testament ones in which the finality of personal death is assumed, that might be of help here in discussing a relation to God unaffected by death, perspectives on personal death that might be extended by us moderns to the whole of the cosmos marked for death?

---

[11] See Bailey, *Biblical Perspectives on Death*, 58–9.

Old Testament passages suggest, first of all, that the dead are not cut off from God because God is the Lord of both life and death. Death is a sphere within God's power, God's reach, and therefore (one presumes) the dead are not lost to God. 'The Lord gave, and the Lord has taken away; blessed be the name of the Lord' (Job 1:21). 'There is no god beside me; I kill and make alive; I wound and I heal' (Deut. 32:39; also, for example, 1 Sam. 2:6–7). Therefore, 'where can I go from your spirit? Or where can I flee from your presence? If I ascend to heaven, you are there; if I make my bed in Sheol, you are there' (Ps. 139:7–8). In keeping with such ideas, maintaining a relationship with the God who gives life would not seem to require the destruction of death (as a more apocalyptic outlook requires). Death does not have the power to separate one from God. Such a confidence, without the development of any explicit ideas about life after death, may underlie Psalms 16, 49, and 73. Thus, in a context where literal death seems to be at issue ['those who are far from you will perish; you put an end (to them)'], the psalmist exclaims, 'my flesh and my heart may fail, but God is the strength of my heart and my portion for ever' (Ps. 73:26).

'Eternal life' (in some of its New Testament senses) develops this suggestion that not even death can separate us from the love of God and others.[12] One with the Word, Jesus is not separated from God on the cross; exactly here (as everywhere else in Jesus' life), the light and life of God enter into darkness and death, to heal and save.[13] In virtue of a continuing union with the Word that death cannot obstruct, the humanity of Christ, as its own powers of life perish on the cross, is able to draw upon the life-giving power of God so as to be resurrected and brought glorified to the Father.[14] United with Christ, we too are inseparable from God: 'Neither death, nor life, nor angels, nor rulers, nor things present, nor things to come, nor powers, nor height, nor depth, nor anything else in creation, will be able to separate us from

---

[12] See, for example, C. H. Dodd, *The Interpretation of the Fourth Gospel* (Cambridge: Cambridge University Press, 1953).

[13] A sharp contrast here with the position of Jürgen Moltmann; see, for example, his *The Crucified God* (San Francisco: HarperCollins, 1991), chapters 5 and 6. For criticism of Moltmann on this score, see Edward Schillebeeckx, *Christ: The Experience of Jesus as Lord* (New York: Crossroad, 1981), 824–5.

[14] See Cyril of Alexandria, *On the Unity of Christ*, trans. J. McGuckin (Crestwood, New York: St Vladimir's Seminary Press, 1995), 125–33.

107

the love of God in Christ Jesus our Lord' (Rom. 8:38). Because we are united with the life-giving humanity of Jesus by the power of the Spirit across the fact of our deaths, as our lives perish of themselves, lose their own powers of living, God gives to us God's own powers of life so as to maintain us. As in the case of Christ's crucifixion, where the divine powers that are always his are put to special use in a victory over death, this life of Christ is also ours now by grace, to be employed by God in a special way at our deaths. In virtue of our relationship to the life-giving powers of Christ's humanity, our lives are lived now, as after death, in and through God's own powers of life: 'I have been crucified with Christ; and it is no longer I who live but it is Christ who lives in me. And the life I now live in the flesh I live by faith in the Son of God, who loved me and gave himself for me' (Gal. 2:19–20). But these life-giving powers of Jesus' humanity do not overcome our deaths until we suffer them, at which time the only power of life we have is God's own.

Because it runs across the fact of death, life in Christ is eternal life. There is a life in the triune God that we possess now and after death, in Christ through the power of the Holy Spirit. Ante and post mortem do not mark any crucial difference with respect to it. Death makes no difference to that life in God in the sense that, despite our deaths, God maintains a relationship with us that continues to be the source of all life-giving benefit. Even when we are alive, we are therefore dead in so far as we are dead to Christ. Separation from Christ (and from one's fellows in Christ) is a kind of death despite the apparent gains that might accrue to one in virtue of an isolated, simply self-concerned existence. Eternal life, moreover, is one's portion or possession despite all the sufferings of life and death in a way that should comfort sufferers of every kind of tribulation. In all the senses of death, including the biological, we therefore live even though we die if we are alive to Christ. 'If we live, we live to the Lord, and if we die, we die to the Lord; so then, whether we live or whether we die, we are the Lord's' (Rom. 14:8).

This understanding of eternal life follows the Old Testament suggestion, then, that all the goods of life ('life' in its extended senses) flow from relationship with God (the second biblical sense of life in relationship): 'ye that did cleave unto the Lord are alive . . . this day'

(Deut. 4:4, KJV). The effort to turn away or separate oneself from God has, in this understanding of things, the force of death, broadly construed. (It is literally the effort to unmake oneself.) Eternal life as *life in God* is a way of indicating this priority of the second biblical sense of life as relationship with God. It is also a way of specifying a character of relationship with God that might survive death. If the world, human society, and individual persons live in virtue of a relationship with God beyond the fact of their deaths, they must live *in* God and not simply in relationship *with* God. After death, the only powers of life our bodies have are God's own powers of life via the life-giving humanity of Christ in the power of the Spirit. *Eternal* life means a deepened affirmation that one's relation with God is not conditional; it is not conditioned even by biological death or the cessation of community and cosmos. The Bible maintains that God remains the God of Israel and the church, remains the God of the world that God creates and of all the individuals in it, whatever happens; the idea of eternal life is simply a way of continuing this affirmation of God's loving and steadfast faithfulness across the fact of death.

While continuing and consummating God's faithful commitment to the creature's good as that is manifest in creation, eternal life is itself a greater gift (and brings in its train greater gifts) than the relationship with God that creatures enjoy simply as creatures. The evident unconditionality of eternal life marks one such difference. With eternal life it becomes clear how relation with God as the source of all benefit cannot be broken by either sin or death (in all its senses including the biological); relations with a life-giving God are maintained unconditionally from God's side. Whatever might happen, God remains faithful to a life-giving relation to us and empowers us, through Christ, for faithfulness, too. The relationship is also unconditional, then, in that what we should be in it – the image of God's own relationship with us – is maintained or shored up from God's side (in virtue of the free favor and mercy of God in Christ) despite our own failings, sufferings, and sin. In the relationship of eternal life, God sets us in and upholds our position in relation to God, whatever we do, whatever happens to us. Despite the fact of human failing, faithlessness and death, we *are* alive in God.

Eternal life is, secondly, not the same sort of relationship as the rather external one that exists between God and creatures: our very identity as creatures is redefined so as to be essentially constituted by relationship with God. Separation from God is now impossible in a way it was not for us simply as creatures. The very meaning of this new identity is that our dependence upon God for our existence is now complete: in Christ we essentially *are* that relationship to God in a way that simply being creatures of God does not entail.

The model for this aspect of life in God is the incarnation. Jesus is the one who lives in God, the one who is all that he is as a human being without existing independently of God, the human being whose very existence is God's own existence – that is the meaning of the hypostatic union. Otherwise expressed, in Jesus God becomes the bearer of our very human acts and attributes. By grace – by virtue, that is, of a life-giving relationship with Jesus that is ours in the power of the Spirit – we enjoy something like the sort of life in God that Jesus lives. We (and the whole world) are to live in God as Jesus does, through him. In short, there is an approximation to the hypostatic union that the world enjoys through grace, most particularly after the world's death, when it transpires that, like Christ, the only life or existence we have is in and through God.

Eternal life is, in the third place, a greater gift than the relations enjoyed simply by creatures because of the gifts it brings with it. As a consequence of the incarnation, the powers and character of Godself shine through Jesus' human acts and attributes – giving Jesus' acts and attributes a salvific force (for example, so as to overcome and heal the consequences of sin) and eventuating in the manifest glorification of Jesus' own human being in the resurrection. So for us, life in Christ brings not just created goods but divine attributes such as imperishability and immortality, which are ours only through the grace of Christ in the resurrection of our bodies. When the fire of our own lives grows cold, we come to burn with God's own flame.

Understood in the way I have been developing, eternal life promotes a more spatialized than temporalized eschatology. The future-oriented eschatology of a future-oriented society here gives way to an eschatology in keeping with the present epoch, which, as Michel

Foucault describes it, is 'the epoch of space. We are in the epoch of simultaneity; we are in the epoch of juxtaposition . . . of the side by side, of the dispersed. . . . [O]ur experience of the world is less that of a long life developing through time than that of a network that connects points and intersects with its own skein.'[15] Eternal life is not the endless extension of present existence into an endless future, but a matter of a new quality of life in God, at the ready, even now infiltrating, seeping into the whole. Eternal life is less a matter of duration than a matter of the mode of one's existence in relation to God, as that caliber of relation shows itself in a new pattern for the whole of life.

At the most fundamental level, eternal life is ours now in union with Christ, as in the future. It is therefore not directly associated with the world's future and not convertible with the idea that the world will always have a future or further time. Here the eschaton cannot be primarily understood as what comes *from* the future to draw the time of this world ever onward.[16] It is not especially associated with any particular moment of time (past, present or future) and therefore such an understanding of the eschaton has no stake in any reworked, theological account of temporal relations in which a coming future is given primacy over present and past times.[17]

Besides the fact that it is not temporally indexed in any of these ways, eternal life is also spatialized in that it suggests a living *in* God, a kind of placement within the life of God. Since there may come a time when the world no longer exists, this placement in God cannot be equated with God's presence or placement within the world.[18] A kind of indwelling of God in us is, however, a consequence of life in God, just as incarnation has as its consequence a human life lived by the power of God. In imitation of Christ, we live in God and therefore the life we lead has a kind of composite character to match our new composite personhood: God's attributes become in some sense our own; they are to shine through our lives in acts that exceed human powers and in that way become established as part of a reborn sense of self. The consequences of that indwelling work themselves out in lives

[15] Michel Foucault, 'Of Other Spaces,' trans. J. Miskowiec, *Diacritics* (Spring 1986): 22.
[16] As both Wolfhart Pannenberg and Jürgen Moltmann suggest.
[17] See, for instance, Moltmann, *Coming of God*, part 4, paragraph 3.
[18] This seems to be the case for Moltmann.

with a temporal flow, but they are being worked out now as much as at any time in the future. Now as after our deaths, there is, moreover, no end to the flow, as a terminal point for religious preoccupation, because as Gregory of Nyssa would have it, the inexhaustible fullness of God's gifts makes itself felt in creatures in the form of an ever-expanding reception of gifts.

Eternal life is also understood in spatial terms so as to become a realm or sphere. Eternal life is a kingdom of God, comparable to an Old Testament sense of righteousness as a new pattern of relationships to which the righteous commit themselves. Eternal life is a new 'power-charged area, into which [humans] are incorporated and thereby empowered to do special deeds.'[19] This realm of eternal life is not other-worldly, either in the sense of becoming a reality only after our deaths or in the sense of a spiritualized, merely personal attitude to events of this world. Instead, eternal life exists now in competition with another potentially all-embracing structure or pattern of existence marked by futility and hopelessness – the realm of death, in the broadest biblical sense of that. One exists in this realm of eternal life now and it extends as far as that other realm of death does, under which, as Paul says, the whole created universe groans (Rom. 8:22). Eternal life infiltrates, then, the present world of suffering and oppression, to bring life, understood as a new pattern or structure of relationships marked by life-giving vitality and renewed purpose.

Eternal life is a present reality; we possess now, in an unconditional fashion, life in God as a source of all good and need not wait for death to pass from the realm of death to that of life. 'He who hears my words and believes . . . has eternal life; he does not come into judgment, but has [already] passed from death to life' (John 5:24). 'So if anyone is in Christ, there is a new creation; everything old has passed away; see everything has become new!' (2 Cor. 5:17). As Bernard Anderson discusses the point:

> [A]lready in the old age people may taste the power of the age to come; already in the old age the leaven of God's kingdom is at work; already in the time of the old creation a new creation is beginning. Thus, the relation between the

---

[19] Gerhard von Rad, *Old Testament Theology*, vol. 1 (New York: Harper & Row, 1962), 376; see also, 388.

two ages . . . is neither a straight-line continuity nor a disjunctive discontinuity. Rather it is continuity and discontinuity. People are called to live in the zone where the circles overlap – where there is discontinuity with the old age even while the old age continues.[20]

Eternal life's present reality does not mean, however, that the full consequences of our entrance into eternal life are evident immediately. Not yet manifest in a world of suffering and tribulation are the full consequences that follow from the decisive fact of eternal life, already ours. A world of blessings – now as after death – are the expected effects of life in God, and therefore life in God permits no simple spiritualization of God's gifts. We and the world are to exhibit all the good consequences of life in God as the signs or manifestations of our entrance into it. 'We . . . have crossed over from death to life; we know this, because we love our brothers. The man who does not love is still in the realm of death' (1 John 3:14–16, NEB). Eternal life is not ours then in a way that suggests there is not more to come in manifestation of it. This 'more,' however, is the world's living out or adequate reflection of what is already the case: this 'more,' for example, is a life with others that properly reflects what follows from life in God, a life in God that has already been granted to us irrevocably from God's side and that exists irrevocably as an empowering source for all the goods of life in its extended senses. After the world's death, when we no longer exist as independent beings apart from God, when we no longer have even an apparent existence outside of God, there must be some different and greater manifestation of such goods in the life we continue to live in God – that is, newness of life, sanctified and imperishable life that carries us beyond the loss of our own powers of living in death.[21]

The model for the life-affirming consequences of life in God is an account of the way the saving effects of Jesus' life and death are enabled by the incarnation. All that Jesus does and 'enjoys' for the sake of life throughout the course of his life and death in a world of sin (healing, delivering, blessing, dying for our sakes) is a consequence

---

[20] Bernard Anderson, *From Creation to New Creation* (Minneapolis: Fortress Press, 1994), 238.

[21] Note that the second coming of Christ might be interpreted here as Christ with all the world alive and sanctified through incorporation in his living body at the world's end.

of his life in God as the incarnate Son of God. What Jesus does and what he suffers are the unfolding of the meaning of life in God (that is, the meaning of incarnation) as that power for life enters into and struggles to overcome a world of suffering, exclusion, and despair. The more that is to come in our lives and the world's (for example, the end of the host of death-dealing consequences of sin) is, similarly, an unrolling or reflection during the time of the world (and after it) of what life in God should bring with it – life in the entirety of its connotations.

In what sense, however, are the goods that properly manifest life in God compatible with the finality of death? Must literal death not be part of the realm of death that eternal life works to overcome? On the cross of Christ, death is taken up into communion with God, thereby proving that death cannot separate us from God. But the consequence of that assumption of death by God is its overcoming, the overcoming of death made clear in the resurrection. Can an understanding of eternal life really conform, therefore, with an Old Testament recognition of death as the end – now not just for individual persons, but for humanity and the cosmos?

Were eternal life understood that way, death might be overcome without requiring the end of mortality. The death that is overcome could, first of all, be simply bad death – the premature, painful, community-rending death, which is the primary Old Testament worry. Death itself, however (in the sense of temporal cessation, in the sense that each of us, the species, and the planet have a limited duration), would remain a simple fact of existence, a concomitant of the finite constitution of things as we know them. In principle, perhaps, eternality (in some sense of that) is not incompatible with finitude, with being a non-divine creature. The fact of the matter, however – following contemporary science rather than, say, an Aristotelian one in which some things (for example, stars and planets) are eternal – is that all organized structures are prone to fail. The world as we know it seems constructed in a way to ensure temporal finitude. We are made from the dust and therefore return to the dust (Gen. 3:19): 'We must all die; we are like water spilled on the ground which cannot be gathered up' (2 Sam. 14:14). 'The earth and the heavens are the work of your hands. They will perish, but you endure; they will all wear out like a garment' (Ps. 102:25–6).[22] As a natural fact about the created world, death could indeed be considered one of the goods of creation. Developing such an idea, one might claim, for example, that the definition of human character requires temporal finitude: If we were never to die, would we be anything in particular? Might not each moment of personal decision lose its character-forming significance if there were always to be a next one?[23] As the Bible suggests, 'So teach us to count our days that we may gain a wise heart' (Ps. 90:12). Certainly on the viewpoint I am developing here, death (as cessation) can be made good. Even Isaiah's vision of the new heaven and earth seems to envision not the end of death but its betterment: 'I create a new heavens and a new earth. . . . No more shall there be in it an infant that lives but a few days, or an old person who does not live out a lifetime, for one who dies at a hundred years will be considered a youth' (Isa. 65:17, 20). Claiming that mortality itself is to be escaped, in a world where, if the scientists are right, the very principles of the universe devolve toward death, suggests Manichaeism. The world seems to be working naturally (certainly before, that is, the entrance of human sin) in a way that runs contrary to God as the source of good.

Bad death in the sense of premature, painful and community-rending death might be overcome by the actions of human beings empowered as givers of the good through life in Christ. Much of what is bad about literal death (its breaking off of relations) and what is therefore bad about death-filled lives (the poverty, disease, discrimination and social exclusions that bring with them forms of isolation and alienation comparable to those of literal death) are overcome in being taken up into God. God's bearing of death (literal and figural) – God's remaining in relation to us in and through death – is the overcoming of death's power to break relations.

The account I have given so far of how death is overcome is not sufficient, however. While it might avoid the tendency to spiritualize

---

[22] This is Athanasius' favorite biblical quotation when arguing for the natural mortality of human beings, in contrast to God's own proper qualities. See his 'Four Discourses against the Arians,' trans. J. H. Newman and A. Robertson, *Nicene and Post-Nicene Fathers*, vol. 4 (Grand Rapids, Michigan: William B. Eerdmans, 1957), 323, 332, 340.
[23] Suggestions like these are developed by Jüngel, *Death*; and by Karl Rahner, *On the Theology of Death* (New York: Herder & Herder, 1961).

bad death found in some theologians like Rahner and Jüngel who accept the natural character of death – bad death for them seems to mean primarily anxious, desperate, untrusting dispositions in the face of death – the account so far does not adequately address the fact of lives that are not made good before death, and of deaths that are in no sense good.[24] If death is simply the end of everything, how can one maintain the expectation of life in God as a fountain of goods in the face of all those creatures whose lives are short and brutish and whose deaths are cruel? Moreover, if we exist in God despite our deaths, the very idea of eternal life suggests some sort of overcoming of mortality itself. But what sort of overcoming of mortality is this, if death remains a creature's good and natural end?

The key to intelligibility here is not to think of our mortality being overcome independently of our life in God. One does do this – one does think of the overcoming of the creature's mortality independently of life in God – when one focuses, as most contemporary eschatology does, on the character of the creature in itself pre- and post-mortem and on the overcoming of mortality as a change in its intrinsic constitution with the transition between the two. This makes eternal life the return of creatures, after the hiatus of death, to something like the existences they had before but now in a form no longer susceptible to death. Although creatures might be said in such a contemporary eschatology to be living in God, independently of that relation they seem to have become immortal themselves.

Avoiding this way of discussing the overcoming of mortality, one can say, instead, that after death (as before death) we are taken up into the life of God as the very mortal creatures we are. It is only in God that we gain immortality; considered independently of this relation to God we remain mortal. We have immortality pre- and post-mortem only in virtue of our relation to an eternal God. Immortality is not, then, granted to the world in the form of some new natural principles that prevent loss or transience; instead, God's own animating eternity shines through or suffuses the very mortal being of those who hold their existence in God. What holds for Christ's own life-giving flesh also holds for the imperishability of our bodies:

[24] See Jüngel, *Death*, 122–33; and Rahner, *On the Theology of Death*, 88.

The flesh of the Lord received the riches of the divine energies through the purest union with the Word, that is to say, the union in subsistence [hypostatic union], without entailing the loss of any of its natural attributes. For it is not in virtue of any energy of its own, but through the Word united to it, that it manifests divine energy: for the flaming steel burns, not because it has been endowed in a physical way with burning energy, but because it has obtained this energy by its union with fire. Wherefore the same flesh was mortal by reason of its own nature and life-giving through its union with the Word in subsistence. [In short] the flesh of men is not in its own nature life-giving . . . [T]he flesh of our Lord which was united in subsistence with God the Word Himself, although it was not exempt from the mortality of its nature, yet became life-giving through its union in subsistence with the Word.[25]

The model for our overcoming of mortality is, then, Christ's own deification. In Christ, human qualities are not elevated in and of themselves beyond what they are capable of as finite. Humanity and divinity remain distinct. Humanity is elevated beyond its capabilities through its union with divinity. It is only as borne by the Word that the humanity of Christ exhibits divine qualities, not in virtue of some new supernatural created powers, not by its becoming more like the Word.[26] In the colorful imagery of Gregory of Nyssa, our bodies are resurrected by the power of God's own life not by way of a change in their nature but in the way the water surrounding a bubble of air is forced upward by it. If such is the case in Christ, then certainly also for us:

For as air is not retained in water when it is dragged down by some weighty body and left in the depth of the water, but rises quickly to its kindred element, while the water is often raised up together with the air in its upward rush, being moulded by the circle of air into a convex shape with a slight and membrane-like surface, so too, when the true Life that underlay the flesh sped up, after the Passion, to itself, the flesh also was raised up with it, being forced upwards from corruption to incorruptibility by the Divine immortality.[27]

[25] John of Damascus, 'Exposition of the Orthodox Faith,' trans. S. Salmond, *Nicene and Post-Nicene Fathers*, vol. 9 (Peabody, Massachusetts: Hendrickson Publishers, 1994), Book 3, chapters 17 and 21.

[26] See Henry Chadwick, 'Eucharist and Christology in the Nestorian Controversy,' *Journal of Theological Studies* 2, part 2 (October 1951): 154, describing Cyril of Alexandria's position on what accounts for Christ's life-giving flesh.

[27] Gregory of Nyssa, 'Against Eunomius,' trans. H. Wilson, *Nicene and Post-Nicene Fathers*, vol. 5 (Peabody, Massachusetts: Hendrickson Publishers, 1994), 181; see also, 179–83. Unfortunately for my purposes, on this same page he uses the vinegar/sea analogy: the flesh takes on immortality the way a drop of vinegar is overwhelmed by the sea.

Indeed, as the early Greek Fathers (Athanasius in particular) affirmed, immortality is not a possible created gift.[28] In paradise (as Athanasius would put it), Adam and Eve were mortal, God simply preventing their deaths as a gift of grace. So too was the humanity of Christ mortal; Jesus genuinely dies on the cross. Mortality is overcome in Christ only in virtue of union with the eternal Son of God; Christ's actual dying makes this clear – that immortality through union with the Word does not become the body's own natural property. Indeed, the less external relationship with God enjoyed by humanity in Christ is the only secure way of overcoming human mortality, if mortality is an intrinsic feature of human life. In the Garden, simply enjoying the relationship of creatures with God, the gift of immortality could be, and in fact was, lost, through sin separating us from God's life-giving power. In that way actual death became the wages of sin, though mortality is not.[29]

If our mortality is overcome as the mortality of Jesus' humanity was, we do not leave our mortal lives behind after death, as if our deaths (and sufferings) have been simply canceled out. We are not replaced by new immortal versions of ourselves, any more than the resurrected Christ appears as someone who is not also visibly the crucified. It is the crucified body that is glorified to immortality in the resurrection of the body. Our mortality is not changed into immortality after death, mortal bodies replaced by essentially immortal ones. Instead, our mortality is (even now, though unapparently) clothed in immortality (1 Cor. 15:33).

This immortality is properly considered ours, despite the fact that we remain mortal in and of ourselves, in so far as, living in God, we are no longer our own but God's. A new identity is in this way given to the world. Not in the form of a new version of one's old nature (considered in itself) but in the transition from an old self-enclosed identity to a new one that is constituted *by* an intimate relationship between who we are (and have been) and the God who offers to mortal creatures something that remains properly God's own. We have this new identity now. We will draw on it, as the life of our own bodies

<hr>

[28] See Athanasius, 'Four Discourses against the Arians,' 323, 326–7, 332, 340.
[29] See Thomas Aquinas, *Summa Theologiae*, trans. Dominican Fathers (Westminster, Maryland: Christian Classics, 1948), IIIa, Q. 14, A. 3, ad 2.

leaves us and as the Word incarnate then gives us his own power of life for our own in a way that makes the life-giving powers of the Word shine through our bodies as the only animating principles they 'possess.'

Clearly, something also happens *to* our mortal lives in and of themselves by virtue of life in God, post-mortem. In God, after its death, the world and everything it has ever contained may really receive as their own, intrinsic properties the blessings of life in God that were perhaps always blocked in the pre-mortem world by forces of sin and death – those forces are no more in God. Immortality may be a gift that creatures cannot receive in themselves without the loss of creature-hood (or the loss of particular identity), and therefore they may have it only in relation to God; but clearly many other gifts stemming from life in God can be received in a way that genuinely transforms the creature's own nature considered in itself – healing replacing a broken woundedness, joy replacing sorrow, justice replacing trials and woes. The life that continues to receive such gifts after death is, however, a life of the world redefined so as to be inseparable from God.

Action for the World's Betterment

How does the eschatology I am developing stimulate action for the better in this life? It might not seem to do so, for a number of reasons. Because eternal life is an unconditional, already realized possession, nothing we do is necessary to bring it about or to sustain it; this might suggest (erroneously, as I shall argue) that action is not obligated in any way *by* life in God. The present possession of eternal life might also seem to compensate for all other disappointments in a way that would simply reconcile us with them; even when matters could be improved by human action we would not see any need to do so because we already have all that we need simply in virtue of life in God. Finally, hope that sustains action in the face of obstacles and disappointment seems shattered by the world's eventual end; and thereby hope for the future of the world itself seems gone as the primary spur to present action.

While on the viewpoint I am developing one need not deny that the future will be different from the present, criticism of the present is not fueled primarily by the difference between present realities and what one expects the future to bring. Instead, criticism of the present is prompted and complacency about it prevented by a recognition of the disparity between the realm of life and the realm of death as those two realms or powers wrestle for supremacy in the here and now. One is led to see the way the world currently runs as an insufferable, unacceptable affront, not by the disparity between the present and God's coming future, but by the utter disjunction between patterns of injustice, exclusion, and impoverishment, which make up the realm of death, and the new paradigm of existence empowered by life in God as a force working in the present.[30] In short, complacency is ruled out not by a transcendent future but by a transcendent present – by present life in God as the source of goods that the world one lives in fails to match. If liturgy is the place where our life in God becomes present to us, it exists as a protest against the world as it is, fueling an opposition to the world of sin like Jesus'.[31]

The shape of Jesus' life (the mode of Sonship) is this new paradigm of existence struggling in the here and now over the shape of life in the world. We are disgruntled with the world as it is in light of Jesus as our world's future, but rather than coming to us simply from the future, Jesus is the new paradigm of the world's existence already realized (in the past of his own life) and as a present force at work for the good in our lives as Christians. Therefore, 'in Christ even in our present lives we are already seized and determined by our future being.'[32]

Action is the proper response to take with respect to a world that is not the way it should be, because, although human action does not bring about life in God (that is God's unconditional gift to us), human action of a certain sort is what life in God requires of us. This is so, first of all, simply because, as we saw in chapter 3, life in God is not inactive, a resting in God in the form of contemplation or adoration. Life in God fundamentally just means sharing in God's own dynamic trinitarian life of indivisible threefold movement as that dynamism is extended outward to us, to include us, in this triune God's relations

[30] See Schillebeeckx, *Christ*, 821.
[31] Ibid., 836.
[32] Karl Barth, *Church Dogmatics* IV/1, trans. G. W. Bromiley and T. F. Torrance (Edinburgh: T&T Clark, 1956), 116.

with us in Christ. Eternal life means a community of life with God in Christ, a community of action in which we are taken up into Christ's own action for the world. As Jesus does the life-giving work of the Father through the power of the Holy Spirit, we, in virtue of our union with Christ, are to do the same. Eternal life turns attention, then, not just to the benefits we are to receive through Christ – our being healed, purified, elevated by Christ in the power of the Spirit – but to our active participation in Christ's own mission. That participation you might say just is the chief benefit – performing the work of the Father as Jesus did. It is the final benefit in that it is what all the others enable. Once healed, purified and elevated, we are perfected so as to participate actively in Christ's mission for the world, no longer simply responding to what God does for and to us but in perfect conformity with the Son serving the kingdom of righteousness.[33]

In this life, life in God sets a task for us, secondly, as a proper sign or witness to our fellowship with God in Christ: we are to be a holy people and in that way demonstrate through the character of our deeds what it means to be God's own. Eternal life calls for a certain way of living to signal one's willing entrance into the realm of God's life-giving being. Only a particular way of living in this world – living so as to counter suffering, oppression, and division – corresponds to life in God, achieved in Christ.

Thirdly, although everything has already been given to us, in a certain sense everything still remains to be done in conformity with that fact.[34] We have everything we need in Christ to live different lives of righteousness, we have a sure promise and firm foundation for another kind of life in Christ. What remains outstanding is growth in openness to this gift and growth in living a life that shows throughout its course the pattern of that gift. Just as the fact of incarnation needed to be worked out in Jesus' life, through the entrance of divine powers within human life and their transformation of it, so our union with Christ needs to be worked out in ours, in an even more difficult struggle against active sin in our own lives and outside them. The more to come, the consummation of our lives in Christ, is the parallel in our lives to

[33] Ibid., 111–16.
[34] Schillebeeckx, *Christ*, 514.

the theanthropic operations of Christ's life and their effects – a transformed pattern of human action that exhibits the mode of the Son.

Eternal life amounts to an unconditional imperative to action in that this life in God remains an empowering source of our action for the good, whatever the obstacles and failing of Christians. The imperative to act is also unconditional in that it is not affected by considerations of success. Irrespective of any likelihood that one's actions to better the world will succeed, and even though one knows all one's achievements will come to nothing with the world's end, one is obligated to act simply because this is the only way of living that makes sense in light of one's life in God. This is the only possibility for us given our reality as God's own. Without primary concern for the consequences of one's actions, one acts out of gratitude for the life in God one has been given, one acts out of joyful recognition that a certain course of action is part of those good gifts that stem from a special relationship with God. In this way, non-moral forms of appreciation and response inform a Christian sense of obligation.

In another sense, action is a conditional imperative as well; one is also acting in an attempt to bring about a world that more closely matches the one that life in God should bring. Although eternal life is not conditional on our action, since it is in a primary sense already achieved through God's action in Christ, the blessings in the world that should naturally follow from it are yet in some significant sense conditional in the world as we know it. Blessings flow from life in God but their egress from that source can be blocked by sin, understood as the effort to turn away from relations with the triune God (and one's fellows), the One from whom all goods flow. In this life, action that accords with the life-giving forces of God runs into the obstructions posed by our world as a realm of death – forces promoting impoverishment, suffering, exclusion and injustice. One is called to act to counter such forces in the effort to bring in another kind of life.

This action cannot, moreover, be delayed in hopes of more propitious circumstances to come. Action is present oriented and therefore realistic. One must work with what one has and that means figuring out the present workings of the world, with, for example, the help of the physical and social sciences, in order to intervene as best one can.

Action has an urgency, moreover; every moment counts. As scientists describe it, the world does not have an indefinite extension into the future; nor will a second chance for action come again by way of a future reinstatement of the world now suffering loss. In religious terms, 'the source for every gaze towards the future is life today, in fellowship with God.' Future hopes do not lure us away from a concern with the present; 'the religious depth of the present is in fact the only thing that can offer grounds for [those future hopes].'[35]

Failure to succeed is not, however, a reason for despair.[36] Certainly, if our action is not primarily motivated *by* hopes for success, the failure of those hopes is no cause to give up the fight. But to the extent our hopes *are* for the furthering of God's blessings through our own action, those hopes can be sustained even in the most dire and hopeless of circumstances; one can continue to hope in God, and specifically in God's gift of eternal life since that is not conditioned by those circumstances or by our own failure because of them. The motor of blessings and of our own action to promote them – eternal life – is something already achieved without us, not something our action brings about, and therefore our hopes in it are not subject to disappointment when our actions fail to have the effects we desire. A hope, then, to counter despair in the present comes not from the idea that God himself is the coming future; but from the fact that despite appearances to the contrary in a world of sin, God has in fact already assumed our lives in Godself. What draws our action and the world ever onward is not a future running ahead of us but a steadfast and unshakable rock (Christ) as the source of that movement, the fund and fountain of what should be an ever expanding feast.[37] On the basis of the fact that in Christ we already have all we need to do so, on the basis of the fact that even now we live in God as Christ does through Christ's mercy, we can hope to have done our part before the end of time. Indeed, we can continue to

[35] Ibid., 800.
[36] See Schillebeeckx's very interesting remarks on failure: ibid., 823–32.
[37] See Gregory of Nyssa, *Life of Moses*, trans. A. Malherbe and E. Furguson (New York: Paulist Press, 1978), sections 243–4: 'here the ascent takes place by means of the standing. I mean by this that the firmer and more immovable one remains in the Good, the more he progresses in virtue. . . . [I]f someone, as the Psalmist says, should pull his feet up from the mud of the pit and plant them on the rock (the rock is Christ who is absolute virtue) then the more steadfast and unmoveable . . . he becomes in the Good the faster he completes the course.'

hope in the world's (and our) further benefit after that end comes but this is no hope in the world in itself, for that world ends (and has already ended *as* something in and of itself); it is a hope in the world whose new identity essentially means nothing other than life in God.

Indeed, in the interim before the world ends, for our part we should expect defeat as much as success. One with Christ who in his mission of benefit suffered humiliation and defeat to all appearances at the hands of the powers, we must prefer defeat to success everywhere that such success means being favored by death-dealing forces at work in human life. In keeping, once again, with the way death and life are relativized by a religious sensibility in both Old and New Testaments, better to go to the cross in faithfulness to the mission of a gift-giving God, than to reap the riches of a kingdom of death:

> [T]o be sacrificed is . . . as long as the world remains the world, a far greater achievement than to conquer; for the world is not so perfect that to be victorious *in the world* by adaptation to the world does not involve a dubious mixture of the world's paltriness. To be victorious in the world is like becoming something great in the world; ordinarily to become something great in the world is a dubious matter, because the world is not so excellent that its judgment of greatness unequivocally has great significance – except as unconscious sarcasm.[38]

---

[38] Søren Kierkegaard, *Works of Love*, trans. H. and E. Hong (New York: Harper & Row, 1962), 288.

Index

125

BOR

Author: BORDOLOI

SERVICE MANAGEMENT (RRMCG)

2019   9781259784637   N : 019194058   U : 019194066

Used In : MGT 4320

Edition : 9th

RENT Due Date : December 20, 2021

		BUY	
NEW	**$70.00**	NEW	$280.00
USED	**$70.00**	USED	$210.00
DIGITAL		DIGITAL	
BryteWave (180 days)	$64.00	BryteWave	$100.00
BryteWave (360 days)	$80.00		

Rent and SAVE up to **$210.00!**

07/01/2021   Book Class 1   1/1 FALL 2021   Tag 1 of 1

sin
consequences of, 15, 32, 37, 46, 61,
69, 76, 86, 109–10, 114, 122
forgiveness of, 56
kingdom of, 28, 59, 119–20, 123
nature of, 2, 2 n.2, 44 n.33, 46, 77, 122
overcoming of, 15, 59, 74, 87, 110
and punishment, 86–7, 86 n.39
in relation to death, 29, 30, 31, 86, 86
n.39, 98, 118
See also humans, as sinners
Sokolowski, R., 5 n.6, 11 n.16
Son (second Person of the Trinity),
14–15, 25 n.55, 25–6, 39, 40, 41, 44
n.32, 54
as image of Father, 14, 40, 41, 54
Sonship, meaning of, 67 n.1. *See also*
Jesus Christ, mode of existence of;
see also under humans, activity of
soteriology. *See* atonement; salvation
Staniloae, D., 14 n.26, 40 nn.18–19, 46
n.39, 53 n.58, 77 n.26, 82 n.34, 83
n.36
Stickleberger, H., 25 n.53
suffering. *See* humans, suffering of;
Jesus Christ, suffering of

Tanner, K., 2 n.3, 3 n.4, 20 n.40, 68 n.2
theodicy, 81
theology
academic, xiii, xvii–xviii
and ethics, xiv–xv, 67
in everyday Christian life, xiii–xvi
feminist, 29
political, 103
process, 10 n.15, 23
and scientific description, 98–103,
114, 122
systematic, xiii, xv, 1
tasks of, xiii–xvi
womanist, 29
Torrance, T. F., 25 n.53, 29 n.64, 47
n.42, 54 nn.60 and 62, 62 n.79
transcendence. *See* God, transcendence
of
transfiguration, 37, 71 n.10

Trigo, P., 80 nn.31–2, 81 n.33
Trinity, 13–14, 35–6, 38–41, 53, 90, 92,
93
and Christian experience, 62, 120–1
distinction between substance and
hypostasis in, 12, 38–9, 41
Cappadocian view of, 38 n.11
as dynamic life, 35–6, 40, 41, 53, 62,
70, 120
as indivisible, 38, 40, 44, 44 n.31, 48,
51–2, 70, 83
as making possible relations with non-
divine world, 13–14
as model for society, 59, 77–83, 95,
121
and non-sexist language, 13 n.22
and relations among the Persons,
13–14, 19, 38–41, 47, 78, 82, 85, 89,
90–1, 92
as co-inherent, 23, 38–9, 43, 43
n.30
as different from fellowship, 51–2,
83
as different from Jesus' relation to
Father, 52
as different from Jesus' relation to
Word, 47
as different from relations among
humans, 40–1, 45–6, 50–1, 82,
95
as different from relationship
between God and world, 41–4
as superabundant, 13–14, 68, 69, 71
unity of, 13, 38–41, 47, 49
work *ad extra* of, 40–1, 52 n.54, 53–4,
70, 91
See also Father; Holy Spirit; Jesus
Christ, in relation to Trinity; Son

Volf, M., 100 n.4

Weber, M., 80
Webster, J., 54 n.61, 61 n.78, 72 n.11
Weinandy, T., 10 n.15
Welch, C., 52 n.53, 62 n.81, 82 n.35
Westermann, C., 80 n.31

CPSIA information can be obtained
at www.ICGtesting.com
Printed in the USA
BVHW050838210522
637698BV00022B/332

9 780800 632939